The Unthinkable Swift

The Unthinkable Swift

The Spontaneous Philosophy of a Church of England Man

WARREN MONTAG

VERSO

London · New York

First published by Verso 1994
© Warren Montag 1994
All rights reserved

Verso
UK: 6 Meard Street, London W1V 3HR
USA: 29 West 35th Street, New York, NY 10001-2291
Verso is the imprint of New Left Books

British Library Cataloguing in Publication Data
A catalogue record for this book is available from the British Library

Library of Congress Cataloging-in-Publication Data
A catalogue record for this book is available from the Library of Congress

ISBN 1–85984–900–8
ISBN 1–85984–000–0 (pbk)

Typeset in Monotype Baskerville
by Lucy Morton, London SE12

Printed and bound in Great Britain
by Biddles Ltd, Guildford and King's Lynn

For Dolores Trevizo
and to the memory of Oscar Martín Trevizo

Contents

Acknowledgements

I must begin by thanking Mike Davis: without his encouragement and constant support this book might well have remained unwritten. Michael Sprinker made invaluable suggestions for its structure at a very early stage of its composition and prodded me along in his inimitable fashion for the duration. Etienne Balibar and Pierre Macherey have been my teachers in every meaningful sense of the term although I was never formally a student of theirs, merely *un élève lointain*: their influence will be obvious to the reader. Ted Stolze and Herb Patterson placed their erudition at my service and called to my attention works in philosophy and history that I might never have discovered on my own. My colleagues in the Department of English and Comparative Literary Studies at Occidental College have provided an irreplaceable atmosphere of friendship and mutual support. David Axeen, Dean of Faculty, was extraordinarily supportive and encouraging. Jean Viggiano's editorial assistance was immeasurably helpful. Desirée Henderson checked the manuscript with great care and helped with the final corrections. Dian Teigler and Chenai Nziramasanga of the Occidental College Library were extremely kind and helpful in the face of my many demands. Finally, I must acknowledge Dolores Trevizo, whose discussions and, yes, arguments with me over our kitchen table have certainly helped shape this work and exposed me to the rigor of a discipline not my own.

1

"All the Contradictions of a Poisoned Age"

Just as one does not judge an individual by what he thinks about himself, so one cannot judge such a period of transition by its consciousness, but, on the contrary, this consciousness must be explained from the contradictions of material life.

KARL MARX, "Preface", *A Contribution to the Critique of Political Economy*

Jonathan Swift's *oeuvre* remains the site of an interpretive battle of the books. The possibility of determining the meaning (in the most basic sense) of works like *A Tale of a Tub* and *Gulliver's Travels* seems less likely than ever, as basic critical divergences now appear inescapable and irreducible. Perhaps even more striking is our apparent inability to answer with certainty the simplest questions about Swift's political beliefs, to decide whether he was a Lockean liberal who conceived of political authority as grounded in the consent of individual subjects (Ehrenpreis 1962, 142; Downie 1985) or a Tory authoritarian who saw society as an organic hierarchy (Lock 1983; Kramnick 1968). In part, these divergences can be (and have been) explained by Swift's peculiar penchant for self-concealment (and not only in his literary works: his most effective political writing concerning the two most important issues of his career – the defense of the Anglican Church's monopoly on religious life and Anglo-Irish sovereignty – makes use of a strategy of ironic impersonation): he not only preferred to publish anonymously, but his views remained carefully concealed behind layers of irony. He impersonated so many speakers representing so many different doctrines that his own views often seem undiscoverable. In fact, some of the best writing on Swift, like Irvin Ehrenpreis's three-volume biography, abets this self-concealment by presenting us with a mass of what sometimes appear to be contingent facts, the very quantity of which discourages us from finding or even seeking answers to the simplest questions about Swift's thought.[1]

If, however, we would understand the necessity that governs the very complexity of his work, its internal divergences (which I take to be irreducible but nonetheless explicable), we must begin with the recognition that this complexity exceeds the dimension of authorial choice (the choice of technique, style, strategy) and is therefore not merely the effect of Swift's cunning or genius: it is historically determined, and as such imposed on Swift as the inescapable condition of his writing.[2] The complexity of Swift's work, its often paradoxical and self-subverting character, is a consequence of its inscription in the uneven and contradictory development of English society (and its Irish colony) during his time and, more precisely, Swift's place as a "Church of England Man" in the most concentrated expression of this radically heterogeneous and therefore overdetermined historical process: the long crisis of the English state. A caesura punctuated the history of England, intervening between the final failure of absolutism in 1688 and the emergence of the modern state in the period after 1714. And it punctuated Swift's life and work as well: this caesura was a time of a deferred recognition (or of a recognition isolated from but coexisting with his "doctrine") of a historical reality that was profoundly unacceptable to him: a capitalist society and an emerging colonial empire presided over by what was, if not a homogeneously capitalist state, a state that finally permitted capitalist development on a massive scale (Hill 1980).

We need to be very clear about what this means (in itself, as well as for Swift, who was by no means anti-capitalist, even if he opposed certain of the effects of capitalism). Every decade that followed the "revolution" of 1688 (and the decades that followed brought enormous economic and political development) (Hill 1972; Plumb 1967) marked an ever-widening gap between the reality of English society and what Swift believed it ought to be. The very progress that a contemporary like Daniel Defoe could hail with a sense of pride and accomplishment in *A Tour Through the Whole Island of Great Britain*, the rise of commerce and the beginnings of industry, attended by greater geographical and social mobility, appeared to Swift (at least in its unforeseen effects) as monstrous, not so much developments as mutations, deviations from a natural order that his theology told him was everlasting and unchangeable (Ross 1941). Swift's literary work – which will comprise the object of this study – is in no sense an external commentary upon or a (perhaps imperfect) attempt to represent this exceedingly complex history; rather, it is a part of this history and, as such, embodies and, despite itself (that is, despite Swift's efforts to master the contradictions of his historical position), displays the conflicts and antagonisms that rendered this conjuncture so unstable and volatile. It is this fact that has made it so difficult to determine Swift's reading of his own historical moment or even to deduce from his life and work a political doctrine, "Swift's politics" (if we believe that his views remained essentially unchanged) or doctrines (if we believe that his views shifted or evolved). The fact that Swift (along with so many of his contemporaries) chose satire as a mode of literary expression and preferred ironic impersonation to speaking *in propria persona* (to a significantly greater extent than others) explains very little: it is rather this fact itself that needs to be explained. Why was it so difficult for Swift to speak in his own voice? To what extent was his recourse to impersonation a necessity imposed on him rather than a choice freely made (the results of which we are first to identify and then to admire)? A response to these questions is not to be found in the works themselves, by interpreting them more carefully or attentively than previous readers, nor in an indifferent exterior to which Swift's works might be only mechanically related. On the contrary, these questions require us to move from inside the works to the outside, but their outside, that which makes them what they are and no other, the conditions of their singular existence.

Such a task, however necessary it may be, has proved difficult and for good reason. Swift's life (1667–1745) encompasses one of the most tormented and complex periods in English history. It is true that the state that ultimately emerged from this crucible (a state that Swift felt was by its essence corrupt, as if it somehow did not correspond to the "civil society" over which it presided) made possible for the first time in well over a century the political stability necessary to economic development at home and political and economic ascendancy internationally (Plumb 1967).[3] The stability achieved was within the ruling classes whose crippling divisions had been overcome; the subaltern classes continued to struggle, although with none of the successes of the 1640s (Thompson 1978). But, as every student of English history knows,

3

this state did not evolve automatically out of the economic and social conditions to which it "corresponded". Rather, it was the outcome of more than a century of struggle, revolution and civil war (and thus in no way preordained or inevitable, a necessary stage in a teleology of progress): a century in which the balance of social forces impeded both the development of an absolutist state and the stabilization of a parliamentary alternative.

In no sense does this history form a hazy background to Swift's life and work. On the contrary, the "horrid rebellion" (as he habitually called it) of 1642, the revolution settlement of 1689, and the last four years of Queen Anne's reign (1710–14) during which the final experiment in Tory rule during Swift's lifetime took place, remained the central reference points of his political thought.[4] In part, this can be explained by biographical fact. Swift's family had been staunchly royalist during the Civil War, and, according to him, suffered grievously for their devotion to the king (*Prose Works* Vol. 5, 188–90). In 1689, Swift, as an Anglo-Colonial Protestant in Dublin, was forced to flee the Catholic army of General Tyrconnel, mobilized in support of the deposed James II. And finally, his years as propagandist of the Tory ministry of Harley and Bolingbroke formed the apex of his career and power. But beyond the specificity of his personal history, it was Swift's position in what remained, precariously or not, an ideological state apparatus (at once an instrument and expression of inter- and intra-class struggles), the Anglican Church (specifically its colonial outpost, the Church of Ireland), that determined and made inescapable his participation in the struggles to make or remake the British state. Swift very accurately defined himself as a Church of England man: he saw history through the eyes of this institution; its tragedies and joys were his own (Landa 1954). When he waged battle, as he did so often and on so many fields, it was usually the Church (whether in its visible or spiritual existence) that was at stake.[5] From freethinking Atheism to efforts to reduce the Church to a merely voluntary association, from moderate Tories to radical Whigs, its enemies were legion. But even more, Swift carried the burden of its history and all the weight of its contradictions and conflicts. It is precisely this "history" (although one hesitates to use the singular) that erupts within works like *A Tale of a Tub* and *Gulliver's Travels*, disfiguring them, not only depriving them of their projected coherence (and with it the factitious interiority that they seem to enclose), but in its violence constituting them in their determinate disorder – their very interiority is a function of the historical exterior.

Before we can understand the development and functioning of the Anglican Church an as ideological state apparatus, however, it is necessary to review the history that enveloped it, a history that Christopher Hill has called "the century of revolution". We may begin with the era that marked the high point of the Anglican Church's power and prestige. Charles I's experiment in absolute rule from 1629 to 1640 (the so-called eleven years' tyranny, during which parliament did not meet) proved fiscally untenable when faced with a military challenge by the Scots. Forced to call parliament in order to raise money, Charles found that he had alienated the quasi-totality of the political nation. The Long Parliament demanded such restrictions on the monarchy and such reforms of the state that Charles I was forced into civil war from 1642 to 1649. The disintegration of the monarchical state, together with parliament's military reliance on the urban masses, resulted in a general radicalization. Traditional forms of authority were called into question, as were, at the extreme, notions of private property. The radicalization, culminating in the execution of the king, frightened the ruling classes, who gradually withdrew their support from parliament and began during the 1650s to mobilize in support of a return of the monarchy. The attempts to construct a new state (commonwealth or protectorate) failed and in 1660 the Stuart monarchy was restored. The restoration brought the so-called "Cavalier" parliament, which passed a series of laws strengthening the church and state. These same laws not long afterwards provoked the Exclusion crisis (1678–81) which featured a renewed attack on the monarchy by parliament (and gave rise to the two parties: the Tories, supporters of the monarchy, and the Whigs, who favored the supremacy of parliament). Following the defeat of the Exclusionists, a new round of authoritarian and persecutory laws were passed and Charles's brother James (who assumed the throne in 1685) attempted to construct an absolutist regime based on a close alliance with France and a revival of Catholicism. This rash course left James isolated and by 1688 the political nation rallied behind the attempt to depose him by an army led by the Dutch king William.

Under William III there began a transformation of the state (as well as society itself) that made absolutism highly unlikely. This new state facilitated Britain's economic development both

5

domestically and internationally. Accordingly, the 1690s witnessed a financial revolution and Britain entered into a long series of continental wars to secure world commercial supremacy. During this period, the Whig and Tory parties underwent significant transformations. The Whig Party, apart from one important interruption, became the quasi-official party of the state and fought to extend the power of the executive. The Tories, after a brief period in power (1710–14), were forced into permanent opposition, paradoxically employing old Whig arguments in defense of parliament, only now against an oligarchy led by Prime Minister Robert Walpole. The social forces that were the base of the Tory Party were either won over to the Whig cause or politically neutralized.

The fact that Swift spent most of his life in Ireland renders this history more rather than less relevant to an understanding of his work. For the fate of Ireland, then a English colony, was inextricably bound up with that of England. The relative fragility of the English hold on Ireland only magnified the effects of the succeeding crises of the seventeenth century on the Anglo-Colonial community to which Swift belonged. Thus in 1641 the conflict between monarchy and parliament encouraged Catholics to rise against British domination, and Protestant settlers were forced to flee Ireland or retreat to a few fortified garrisons. Immediately following, a rebel assembly, "the confederation of Kilkenny", advanced the idea of a united Catholic nation that would formally recognize the king (and lend him much-needed military support), if it could be guaranteed *de facto* independence. When the Royalist forces were decisively beaten and the king himself was executed in 1649, the English parliament turned its attention to the Irish rebellion. Cromwell's army of thirty thousand experienced soldiers reconquered Ireland in less than a year and imposed a "settlement" that transferred most land to Protestant ownership. Ireland was henceforth governed as a garrison state. It was during this time that Swift's father settled in Ireland, taking advantage of the opportunities afforded by the Cromwellian occupation. The Restoration meant no relief for the Catholic majority and, with some minor exceptions, Cromwell's policies were extended and the confiscations of Catholic property upheld. Opposition among Catholics to colonial rule grew, especially after a wave of persecutions that followed the discovery of the Popish Plot in 1678. They looked to James II as their savior, and he began appointing Catholics to key posts in the state and the military. The most important of these, the Earl of Tyrconnel, was a popular leader whom James appointed Lord Deputy of Ireland in 1687. When James was deposed in 1688, the Catholics rallied to his cause and an army led by Tyrconnel seized control of all but a few fortified towns to which the Protestants had withdrawn. Most Protestants – or, rather, those who (like Swift) could afford to – fled to England in the face of Catholic revolt. James arrived in Ireland and called the last parliament to be dominated by Catholics until the twentieth century. The Patriot Parliament, as it was later called, restored to Catholics lands confiscated since 1641 and instituted an important measure of legal independence for Ireland.

By 1691, however, English and Dutch forces had defeated Tyrconnel's army and Ireland was once again subjugated. It was at this point that the rift between the colonial community and the English government in which Swift was to play an important role developed. English Protestant domination could be assured only if Irish Catholics (who comprised at this time 90 per cent of the population) were permanently disarmed, demobilized and excluded from political life (Johnston 1974, 53). Protestants felt that the Treaty of Limerick, which concluded the Jacobite wars, was too lenient (especially in matters of religion and property) and would not assure their security against an indigenous population of such overwhelming numerical superiority. Not only did they refuse to ratify the treaty until 1697 (by which time most of the offending provisions, namely anything that might uphold the rights of Catholics, had been removed), they also demanded, beginning in 1695, the imposition of the infamous Penal laws which institutionalized their economic as well as political hegemony.

Henceforth, parliament was an exclusively Protestant body by law (within a few decades, Catholics were also deprived of the right to vote). Catholic education was abolished. Pilgrimages and religious processions of any kind were prohibited on the grounds that any gathering of Catholics in large numbers posed a potential threat. Catholics were forbidden to own weapons of any kind and were restricted to owning one horse. They could not buy land, and their ability to bequeath property to their children was severely restricted. The result was that by the end of the 1720s, the Catholic population (estimated at that time to be between 75 and 80 per cent of the population) owned 10 per cent of the land, had not a single member of parliament or government official of any kind, and could not vote. Persecuted and impoverished, as

7

politically "inconsiderable as the women and children", as Swift put it (1963, Vol. 2, 120), the Catholic majority would pose no threat to the colonial community for decades to come. With British military support seen as largely unnecessary and with the increasing pressure of economic competition, the conflict between the colony and the metropole intensified, and a peculiar "colonial nationalism" (Simms 1976; McCracken 1986) flourished, appropriating to itself the appellation Irish. The already narrow base of the Protestant community was narrowed further when, in 1704, a sacramental test was imposed, excluding the dissenting community (half the Protestant population) from government posts and military command. Economic and political power remained firmly in the hands of Anglican landlords who comprised less than 10 per cent of the island's population. It was for this "nation" that Swift came to play the part of patriot, defending its interests not only against England but against Irish Catholics and dissenters as well.[6]

To render this complex epoch intelligible without reducing its complexity to one of two all-too-familiar alternatives (a teleology of progress or a series of dissociated and indifferent accidents among which would figure the contingent actions of autonomous individuals), we might describe this period as a prolonged bourgeois revolution. Once the notion of bourgeois revolution was thought to apply only to conflicts between a rising (mostly urban) bourgeoisie, perhaps in alliance with a capitalist gentry and a reactionary absolutist monarchy supported by feudal magnates in the countryside. Innumerable criticisms of this model have been advanced, not least because not a single actual transition to capitalism corresponds to it. But this does not automatically invalidate the concept. We may well follow the lead of Nicos Poulantzas and say that there is no universal norm or pure state of bourgeois revolution to which the particular "case" of England may or may not correspond, but only bourgeois revolutions, each characterized by its "conjunctural originality".

Christopher Hill, who himself some fifty years ago described the revolution of the 1640s as corresponding to the classical model, has more recently attempted to recast the concept. He argues that we can speak of a bourgeois revolution in seventeenth-century England not in the sense that a united bourgeoisie, conscious of its interests, squared off against an equally conscious, distinct feudal class, but because the popular masses, led by a force that

8

consisted of the gentry, aristocracy and merchants, destroyed the old patrimonial or quasi-absolutist state "root and branch" in a way that they neither willed nor could have predicted. Their actions had the effect (whatever the causes of these actions, causes that were surely heterogeneous) of establishing "conditions that were far more favorable to the development of capitalism than those which prevailed before 1640" (Hill 1980, 111). And this was equally true for the revolution of 1688. That the entire process was profoundly contradictory, characterized as much by reversals and regressions as by progress, and that it was impelled by social forces which were unable to sustain their unity and could not agree upon the new state to be constructed (whether in 1642, 1678–82 or 1689) does nothing to change the revolutionary character of the transformations that took place:

> What emerged was a state in which the organs that most impeded capitalist development: Star Chamber, High Commission, Court of Wards, and feudal tenures; in which the executive was subordinated to men of property, deprived of control over the judiciary, and yet strengthened in external relations by a powerful navy and the Navigation Act; in which local government was safely and cheaply in the hands of the natural rulers and discipline was imposed on the lower orders by a Church safely subordinated to Parliament. This Church was as different from the Church which Archbishop Laud had wished to see as the state of William III was from the State of Charles I and Strafford, as the culture of Pope, Defoe and Hogarth was from the culture of Beaumont and Fletcher, Lancelot Andrewes and Vandyke. (Hill 1980, 135)

It is not surprising, then, that a process so conflictual, driven by struggles whose stakes were unclear to the forces involved, produced a heteroclite and unevenly developed state. Within this state the old and the new, the anachronistic and the innovative, the vestigial and the functional, coexisted in what was obviously a compromise formation determined by the balance of class and intra-class forces: unlike the Cromwellian state of the 1650s, it simultaneously placated the reactionary social sectors (for whom the preservation of the legal privileges of the Anglican Church was paramount) and allowed the development of capitalism and the colonial empire through new or transformed institutions that the more backward rural sectors (together with certain privileged merchants) might otherwise have more vigorously opposed (particularly the greatly enlarged bureaucracy and the permanent

9

military). It was not, therefore, that the transformation of this state was somehow incomplete,[7] but that the heterogeneity and unevenness specific to it was the necessary condition (which was by no means predetermined) of capitalist development in England during this period.

This unevenness, in turn, gave the period a deceptive character (an observation that is crucial to any understanding of Swift's work), rendering it peculiarly opaque to those who lived it. Of course, this may be said of any epoch, but in the period between 1688 and 1714 it was possible to believe that the old order had not fundamentally changed – that, on the contrary, it had been saved from unwelcome tampering, if not outright destruction, at the hands of a monarch bent on imposing absolutism and Catholicism on an unwilling people. The monarchy, the peerage, the Church, even parliament, were thus felt to have been "restored" (an absurdity given that they were restored to what they had been during a period that was itself called a Restoration, although few of these institutions were in fact restored to what they had been before 1642) and it was far from clear to Swift and his co-thinkers, especially during the Tory heyday of 1710–14, that social forces of overwhelming and irresistible character, international as well as national, were either changing these institutions or modifying the role that they played in the social order.

Swift, like his friend and colleague Francis Atterbury, may have dreamed of restoring to the Church the powers that it possessed in the glorious years of Charles I and Archbishop Laud (Bennett 1975, 20),[8] but he came in time to realize that this, like so many of the hopes of the Tory Party, was, as one historian put it, "utterly futile" and "ridiculously unrealistic" (Plumb 1967, 129). But, as Freud noted in another domain, hopes and dreams do not vanish merely because their impossibility has been demonstrated: they may well, on the contrary, cling all the more tenaciously to life. Even as they are unspeakable, unthinkable, in flagrant contradiction to all that exists, they may nevertheless make themselves heard and felt at those sites in which reasoned political and philosophical discourse has no place – say, as the unstated presuppositions of satire, or displaced (and therefore disavowed) to the account of an imaginary voyage. Duped by a prolonged bourgeois revolution that masqueraded as a restoration (or rather as a succession of restorations) and that adopted the appearance of the old order as if to lull its unwitting participants into supporting unprecedented economic and social transformation, Swift found that he had helped bring about the changes that made him an anachronism, truly an *unzeitgemässer Mensch*. Unlike so many of his friends (among them, Harley, Bolingbroke and Atterbury), Swift seems, after the death of Queen Anne (but only then), genuinely to have understood the irreversibility of these changes, regarding as futile (and perhaps undesirable, given the Pretender's continuing adherence to Catholicism) any hope of a Stuart restoration.

Nowhere were the paradoxes of this bourgeois revolution more keenly felt than in the Anglican Church, the condition of which Swift, like many of the clergy, "lived" as a tragically ironic disjunction between appearance and reality, or, as he put it in *The Argument Against Abolishing Christianity*, between the nominal and the real. The Church, ever the focal point of Swift's political efforts (at least before his turn to the concerns of the Anglo-Irish colonial community in the period following 1714),[9] successfully resisted every attempt to break its monopoly on the nation's religious life (even Walpole gave up trying to reduce its powers by the 1720s). But its victory proved over time to have been a hollow one. Church attendance dropped significantly with each succeeding decade; what remained of the once powerful ecclesiastical courts withered away for lack of fiscal support. The Church's powers, such as they were, remained unused and were perhaps unusable. Its theological and philosophical underpinnings were under attack from within as well as from without. A new generation of liberal churchmen sought to modify Anglican theology to make it agree with the new philosophies of nature and society, accepting both material explanations of the natural world and arguments for religious tolerance. The expiration of the Licensing Act in 1695 unleashed a tide of openly atheistic and anti-clerical literature (Bennett 1975, 18) which, because of its grounding in the work of Hobbes and Spinoza, was in certain ways far more forceful and threatening than the sectarian tracts of the Commonwealth days.

To take an example that expressed the paradoxes of the Anglican establishment, one of the cornerstones of its power (and thus a constant concern of Swift's) was the Test Act, originally passed by the Cavalier parliament in 1673 (although it was not imposed in Ireland until 1704) to spite Charles II, whose religious sympathies were already under suspicion. The Test Act required all those who would hold government office to participate regularly in the rituals of the Anglican Church (including the taking of communion) and to produce a certificate signed by an ordained clergyman proving such participation. From the moment of its passage, the Test was the subject of immense controversy in as well as out of parliament, and opposition to it (led by the Whigs) reached a peak in the first decade of the eighteenth century. Opponents argued quite understandably that the Test was simply a form of religious persecution, a hangover from the absolutist state that the early Stuarts had tried to impose on the nation. They argued that freedom of worship and liberty of conscience ought to be enjoyed by all in a nation that claimed to have rid itself once and for all of arbitrary rulers and their episcopal allies.[10] The majority of the political nation, however, especially the rural gentry, feared that religious and political dissent remained as indissolubly allied as they had been in the 1640s and 1650s when religious sects like the Levellers and the more radical Diggers questioned not only religious and secular forms of authority but even the distribution of property and wealth itself.[11] Thus the Church was preserved as a "bulwark against anarchy", that is, as an ideological state apparatus that would help maintain a balance of power favorable to the ruling classes. And while the Church proved to be an effective instrument in preventing the re-emergence of radical religious movements among the plebeian masses, its effect on wealthy dissenters (especially merchant communities in the larger towns and cities) was virtually nil, thanks to a practice known as "occasional conformity", by which a dissenter desirous of holding office or occupying a post as civil servant would take communion in an Anglican Church as "occasionally" as once a year, qualify for his certificate of conformity and be free to worship as he saw fit for the rest of the year. This *de facto* nullification of the Test was especially difficult for the Church of Ireland (the outpost of the Anglican Church in the Irish colony), where Anglican congregations fought a losing battle within the Protestant community against an ever-growing number of dissenting chapels and meeting houses.

It is little wonder, then, that Swift, who spent a great part of his political career defending the Test, argues with bitter irony in his great *Argument Against Abolishing Christianity* (1708) that since the power of the Church is already nominal rather than real, what improvement could possibly result from that abolition of the Test, "an old dormant statute" that has never hindered anyone "in the pursuit of any civil or military employment" (*Prose Works* Vol. 2,

30). Strict enforcement of the Test Act would have had an effect similar to the described effect of the restoration of real as opposed to nominal Christianity in Swift's *Argument Against Abolishing Christianity*: it would have "ruined trade" and turned all the "courts, shops and exchanges into deserts" (30).

But the question remains of how the specific complexity of the Anglican Church determined Swift's views of society and history. For we have not yet addressed the problem of identifying Swift's politics, nor the problem of explaining why this task is itself so problematic. The nature of Swift's writing has not made this task easy. His most successful works, say *The Conduct of the Allies* (1711), which helped build a majority to end Britain's participation in the War of the Spanish Succession, or *The Drapier's Letters* (1724), tend to be very specific in nature, interrupted only occasionally by frustratingly abbreviated statements of general principles which, further, must be sifted from the complexities of the narrative persona and the implied audience to which it addresses itself. The very brevity of these statements, together with the difficulty of abstracting them from the specific historical situation in which they are inscribed, often inhibits rather than facilitates any inquiry into Swift's general political theory.

At the same time, his few general expositions, such as *The Sentiments of a Church of England Man* or the *Project for the Advancement of Religion and the Reformation of Manners* (both of which make explicit the centrality of the Church to Swift's vision of society), constitute some of Swift's least effective work. Written at a time when the political nation faced a crisis of direction as severe as any since 1689 (Plumb), during which Swift wavered between the Whigs and the Tories, these pieces are marked by his attempt to situate himself beyond "the rage of party", to pose as a neutral observer capable of judiciously weighing opposing arguments. But Swift, by "unbiasing his mind as much as possible and then endeavoring to moderate between the rival powers" (*Prose Works* Vol. 2, 121) produces only platitudes about the danger of faction when the bulk of both parties consists of reasonable men devoted to the preservation of Church and State. Further, *The Sentiments of a Church of England Man* attempts to reconcile contradictory ideas and positions on Church and State, as if political liberty were perfectly compatible with the systematic exclusion of dissenting Protestants from political life and the suppression of all theological debate. And it surely does not help clarify "Swift's politics" to learn that a mere three years later he would abandon the role of "moderator" and adopt the position of a Tory extremist to accuse the Whigs of having conceived a "design of destroying the Established Church" and "endeavoring to undermine the present form of government and to build a commonwealth" (*Prose Works* Vol. 2, 142).

In fact, the more closely we examine the supposed consistency of Swift's political views, the greater and more fundamental seem the discrepancies and contradictions that appear. Swift, from the time of his first political essay, *Discourse of the Contests and Dissensions between the Nobles and Commons in Athens and Rome* (1701), to his final essays in the 1730s, advocated a theory of the "balance of power" whereby the three estates, the monarchy, the nobility and the commons, rule together (Ehrenpreis 1962, Vol. 2, 55). This doctrine emerged as a weapon of the opposition to Charles I and even more as the doctrinal centerpiece of the emergent Whig opposition to Charles II and James II in the late 1670s and 1680s. Swift, who was perfectly capable of citing this doctrine against any monarch who flaunted "the will of the people" by threatening to grant toleration to non-conformists (whether the *absolutisant* James II or the limited monarch George I) nevertheless exhibited a very peculiar understanding of the theory. For while many of his contemporaries felt that in no reign was this balance so threatened than in that of Charles I (who, after all, ruled without parliament for eleven years), Swift could praise this king as among the greatest the nation ever had (*Prose Works* Vol. 9, 219–31), even as he vilified the far less powerful Hanoverians as despots and tyrants.

Once we recognize this inconsistency, other hitherto unasked questions emerge. What, for instance, was Swift's attitude towards absolutism and the absolutist state in its various English incarnations? This is hardly an insignificant issue given the allure of Jacobitism among Tories, included among them Swift's closest friends: Harley, Bolingbroke, and Atterbury. And while it is true that Swift voiced his opposition to "arbitrary government" and "divine right" from the beginning to the end of his political career, the reality is more complex. His opponents (after 1710) charged that these statements were aimed at defending himself and the Tory Party against charges of Jacobitism and might thus be disregarded (and his opponents had some grounds for their suspicions given that Harley and Bolingbroke made similar statements even as they were corresponding with the Pretender). There is, however, not the slightest evidence that Swift himself ever placed any hope in a Stuart Restoration. Further, it is quite clear that Swift sincerely despised the last experiment in absolutism, that of James II, for its subversion of the Anglican Church (but of course so did Atterbury, who nevertheless became a Jacobite).

This is where the story ends for most critics. But this does not exhaust the complexity of Swift's views. For these views are incompatible with many of the ideas and sentiments expressed in his political writing during the period 1710–14, and even more with his sermon commemorating the martyrdom of Charles I (1725), in which the most extensive experiment in absolutist rule that Britain was to see is praised in barely qualified terms, and this at a time when some of Swift's closest friends were in exile for conspiring to restore Charles's grandson to the throne. In his sermon, Swift emerges as an unashamed admirer not only of the monarch under whose rule the Anglican Church reached the zenith of its powers, but also of two principal architects of this nearly absolutist regime, Strafford and Archbishop Laud (who through the then powerful ecclesiastical courts carried on the most extensive campaign of persecution against religious dissidence in the history of the Anglican Church). This generally overlooked document constitutes one of Swift's most sustained expositions on the British state in the seventeenth century (Rosenheim 1976; Lock 1983). The sermon is not simply an attack on parliament for having "destroyed church and state" (*Prose Works* Vol. 9, 224). It is in fact a forceful defense of absolutist institutions, from the ecclesiastical courts of Laud to the infamous Star Chamber, perhaps the key instrument of royal prerogative (although Swift admits that the latter had suffered some corruptions). This defense of monarchy is all the more significant given that it was delivered during the reign of a monarch that Swift thought utterly corrupt and tyrannical.[12] Even more revealing than Swift's meditation on the past are his arguments, during the last four years of Anne's reign, for extending the royal prerogative. As Herbert Davis notes, Swift found it prudent to remove these passages when his works were reprinted during the reign of George II lest they be used by Whigs in support of "their" monarch (*Prose Works* Vol. 3, xxviii). Scattered throughout Swift's writings, at odds with his statements of political principle, his historical commentary, as well as his defense of the Tory ministry from 1710–14 (which constantly refers back to the Queen's martyred grandfather and to the "fanatics" and "dreaming saints" who were responsible for his overthrow and execution) disrupts and calls into question Swift's own conceptualization of his political positions.

Swift shared with his High Church brethren a central, inescapable contradiction that made many of them embrace the Jacobite cause, even though it meant restoring a Catholic monarch to the throne. How could such apparent folly have been so widespread? The positions of the High Church Tories were hopeless precisely because the Church they envisioned was more compatible with an absolutist regime than with a constitutional monarchy given the relation of social forces in eighteenth-century Britain. But how do we explain, in the light of his apparent denunciations of absolutism, Swift's lifelong attempts to restore the Church to what it was (both *de jure* and *de facto*) and could only be as an apparatus of an absolutist state?

Swift's writing provides few clues. His other efforts to address the major questions of Church and State on a more abstract level, such as his "Remarks" on Matthew Tindal's *Rights of the Christian Church Asserted*, as well as his numerous attempts at historical writing, remained mere fragments. Even his efforts to reflect on his own experience in the period 1710–14 remained, as Ehrenpreis noted, "incomplete or unpublishable" (1962, Vol. III, 445). It appears that Swift was incapable of producing a sustained, reasoned exposition of his political "world-view" in general, and equally incapable of gathering the diverse facts and events of a specific historical period into a coherent narrative. This inhibition that blocked Swift's writing, or set it in conflict with itself, poses crucial problems for the analysis of Swift's *oeuvre*. For his unspoken, and perhaps unspeakable, political, religious and philosophical ideas ("fantasies" might be a better term) shaped Swift's literary, clerical and political career. It will be objected that the most important expositions of Swift's views were his literary works (especially *A Tale* and *Gulliver's Travels*), and in a very real sense this is undoubtedly true. However, that Swift was all but incapable of explaining his views in positive form and could only allude to them negatively in his satires, or put them in the mouths of characters whose authority and pertinence to Swift's audience is determined in very complex ways, is surely deserving of explanation. The opposing accounts of Swift's political and philosophical beliefs are thus not errors of interpretation at all: the critical conflict itself is objectively determined by Swift's writing, by its confusion and prevarication, by its seemingly unwitting presentation of mutually exclusive positions. The confusion, however, was not merely Swift's. His writing is not so much determined by a set of guiding ideas as by the institution in relation to which he defined himself (and, even more, to be situated at its weakest point, the Church of Ireland) and within which his writings are indissociably inscribed, and this institution was from its origins confused, radically disarticulated and riven with contradictions.

Nowhere else in Europe was the Reformation so little motivated by religious passion from below and so openly an element of policy, dictated by economic necessity. The great Anglican apologetics appeared more than fifty years after the Reformation, as Richard Hooker and Lancelot Andrewes attempted to supply a retrospective justification both of the break with the Roman Church and of the refusal to reform very much. Of course, the fact that no ideological formation preceded the institutional break, furnishing the idea that the reality might strive to emulate, did much to undermine the Church's claims to legitimacy. Further, Henry VIII seemed to have rescued the Church from Rome only to destroy it, alternately encouraging Calvinists when their program of austerity suited his own and repressing them when they appeared seriously to threaten what was still an important apparatus of domination, one that neither Henry nor subsequent kings for many generations could do without. The first decade of the Reformation in England was immensely destructive to the political power as well as to the infrastructure of the Church (which at this time remained essentially Catholic despite its independence from Rome), and the instrument of destruction was parliament. Parliamentary acts made the king "supreme head" of the English Church, permitted the Crown to tax the Church (the Act of First Fruits and Tenths, an act that Swift spent a good deal of his political career trying to circumvent). Resistance to these attempts to strengthen royal supremacy (the Lincolnshire rising and the Pilgrimage of Grace) ultimately served only to stimulate its further extension: all monasteries were made property of the Crown by act of parliament. Rather than transferring them for the use of the new Church, the monasteries and all the wealth they contained (jewels, plate bullion, and so on) were rapidly liquidated, creating a new landowning class with a decided material interest in permanently ridding England of Popery. The Henrician Reformation did not stop there: whatever bridges might lead back to

17

Rome were destroyed. Books, documents, icons and images, together with entire edifices, were destroyed. A reformed Church thus ravaged, lacking sound doctrine, was ill positioned to serve as an ideological apparatus. In fact, the tide of those who wished to see even greater reforms to purify the Church was rising. The plebeian social base of incipient Puritanism, together with its anti-authoritarian tendencies which had already led to numerous social disturbances (Cross 1976, 77–8), made this movement unaccept-able to the Tudors and led to the formation of the Church–State alliance – as necessary to the early phases of absolutism as it was destructive to the more ambitious Stuart project of the early seventeenth century. With the Act of Six Articles in 1539, the slow and uneven process of restoring to the Church certain juridical functions began. With the passage of the Supremacy and Uni-formity Acts by parliament under Elizabeth, Church doctrine, as well as its "visible" form, were established. In none of this was the Church consulted: its law-making body, the Convocation, played no role in the key moments of the Reformation. The vast major-ity of the clergy simply acquiesced in the transformation. From this moment on, the Church, both institutionally and doctrinally, was tied to the Crown and therefore to the troubled and discon-tinuous absolutisms of the agonized century that was to follow.

Tudor policy towards the Church had two objectives: (i) To sever the connection to Rome as a step towards the establishing of the sovereign nation-state; (ii) to deploy this retooled institution as an apparatus of the new state. But such a policy was under-mined itself in a number of crucial ways. First, the break with Rome was initially undertaken on solely political (and not doctri-nal) grounds. Henry VII had no desire to change Catholic doc-trine and sought rather to function as Pope himself. But such a move, precisely because of its limited character, failed both to win the approbation of Protestants, who pushed for a reformation, and the support of Catholics, such as Thomas More, who could see no doctrinal justification for Henry's policy. Further, the spe-cific form of the subordination of the Church to the state, the fact that Church organization and doctrine were established by acts of parliament (and this was true during the Henrician and Edward-ian Reformations, the return to Rome under Mary, and finally the Elizabethan settlement), made arguments for the divine character of the Church very difficult. Indeed it was all too easy to argue as Matthew Tindal did (to Swift's chagrin) that the Church was "a perfect creature of civil power" (*Prose Works* Vol. 2, 71), an artificial, not natural, thing that might be changed at any time as easily as it was brought into being, by act of parliament. As we have noted, the financial subordination of the Church to the state had an even more destructive effect on the institutionality of the Church. Governed by a relationship of forces that made it impossible to tax the gentry and nobility (and this despite their growing wealth), Henry and Elizabeth were forced to liquidate the Church holdings that they now controlled. The limitations of the English monarchy forced it to enlarge itself at the expense of the Church, with fatal consequences for both the monarchical and ecclesiastical establishments.[13]

At the same time, the monarchy could not do without the Church as an ideological and repressive apparatus of the state. But the limited nature of the doctrinal breach with Rome, together with the persecution of Protestants that often accompanied Henry's self-limiting revolution, undermined the ideological authority of a Church that was neither Catholic nor reformed, lacking until Elizabeth's reign any institutional uniformity. Even more damagingly, the great philosophical foundation of the Church, Hooker's *The Laws of Ecclesiastical Polity*, did not appear until the end of Elizabeth's reign, sixty years after the inauguration of the Reformation in England and a mere fifty years before the abolition of the Church by parliament. Hooker's eloquent and learned arguments for the Anglican compromise, his attempts to ground Church practice in the primitiveness of the apostolic Church, thereby granting Anglicanism the original divinity that its Puritan critics denied it, were too little and too late. Based on the scholastic Aristotelianism that served Aquinas so well, the very philosophical underpinnings of Hooker's enterprise were soon to be nullified by the effects of astronomy, physics and mathematics in the philosophical field (Bacon, Descartes, Hobbes and the Epicurean revival). Similarly, formidable barriers blocked the expansion of the Church's coercive powers. In particular, the capitalist landlords in the countryside counterposed their own power to that of the Church, particularly in the judicial realm, resented ecclesiastical taxes, and generally supported a more thorough Reformation. Various forms of Puritanism took root in this rising social class, all of which shared a demand to abbreviate Church institutions, a demand in which fiscal and religious concerns happily coincided. A unified Church was deemed unnecessary, as indeed it was from the point of view of their material interest in the context of a very specific historical conjuncture. When the conjuncture changed, as it did beginning in the 1640s, this same class, alarmed at the unforeseen consequences of the abolition of the monarchy and Church, would rally to the cause of both, demanding and sincerely celebrating the restoration of the very institutions they helped overthrow.

The Tudor Reformation thus conferred upon the Anglican Church its seemingly contingent character: barely differentiated from the Roman Church in some respects and from Calvinism in others, it appeared as a hybrid and an amalgam.[14] The statist character of the Reformation, the corresponding failure early on to provide sustained and convincing doctrinal justification of the specific form of the Reformation, compelled Elizabeth to seek to define a Church comprehensive enough to unite all the factions in a single national entity, an effort doomed utterly to failure. Lacking a stable institutional base, appearing alternately as a Catholic Church pared to the quick and an incompletely reformed Reformation Church, the *via media* was often little more than an incoherent compromise, designed to satisfy so many competing interests that it could only end by failing to satisfy any of them. Its very existence was at stake in the debates over the precise vestments to be worn by the priest or the disposition of furniture and bodies in the space of the church. The boldness with which the Church announced its own materiality offended many at a time when the infinite inwardness of the individual subject had begun to shape the spirituality proper to the early modern epoch. Seemingly more concerned with the precise disposition of bodies than with the souls that inhabited them, with the pronunciation of certain words than the motives and intentions that determined this pronunciation, in short with the visible, material world rather than with the invisible spiritual world, the Church appeared more an instrument of policy than a house of God and a community of the faithful.

It is easy to see, given the nature of the Anglican Reformation, why Swift would find it difficult to discuss coherently and at length his reading of this Reformation, the resonances of which shaped many of the political and even philosophical debates of his time. Swift was far from uninterested in the Reformation: quite the opposite (Landa 1954, 160–64). It was a major focus of much of his reading. But his commentary on this decisive historical moment

is scattered through his works in the form of marginalia or parenthetical statements without ever assuming coherent form. His
responses to Whig adversaries, such as the Deist Matthew Tindal
or the Whig Bishop Gilbert Burnet, tend to avoid larger historical
questions. But Swift could not entirely avoid them: in fact he
produced one of the most famous commentaries on the Reformation of his time, if a literary satire whose meaning and allegiance
was far from clear could indeed be called a commentary (Harth
1961). The complexity of *A Tale of a Tub*, in particular the distance
between Swift's stated intentions and the actual effects produced
by the work (to be discussed in the next chapter), is indissociable
from the institutional history of the Anglican Church, from its
origins a too transparent instrument of policy.

With the accession of James I in 1603, which Swift regarded as
a blessing (Landa 1954, 160), the Stuarts, faced with a dual crisis
of Church and State, set about constructing a genuine absolutism.
Without recourse to the various temporary financial expedients
(for example, the sale of seized Church property) that allowed the
Tudors to strengthen the monarchy and even moderately to expand its administrative apparatus without directly confronting the
landowning classes (whose taxes were one-quarter of what their
French counterparts paid), the Stuarts were forced into a confrontation in the most unfavorable of circumstances.

In his attempt to set about constructing a real absolutism, James
I chose to begin by strengthening the ideological apparatuses of
the state rather than by extending in practice the reach of royal
prerogative. His administration began to issue judgments upholding the power of the king independent of the will of parliament.
But more importantly (and fatefully), he began his reign almost
immediately by declaring an alliance with the Church against
Catholics, and even more importantly against the Puritans. On his
way to London in 1603, James was presented with the Millenary
Petition, a moderate document signed by a thousand conforming
ministers who asked for a number of popular reforms (more
restricted use of excommunication and other forms of discipline,
the abolition of the sign of the cross in baptism and the ring in
marriage) the adoption of which would have given the Church a
far broader base. Hoping that the king's acquaintance with Scottish Presbyterianism would make him more sympathetic to the
Puritan cause and less committed to the established institutions of
the Anglican Church, the Puritans were sorely disappointed. James

called a conference at Hampton Court to settle the matter and personally intervened to strengthen the position of the Anglican Church against its Puritan critics. Proposals to weaken or dilute the authority of the Episcopate were met with James's famous admonition:

> If you aim at a Scottish Presbytery, it agreeth as well with monarchy, as God and the devil ... No Bishop, no king ... If this be all your party hath to say, I will make them conform themselves, or else I will harrie them out of the land, or else do worse. (cited in Gwatkin 1917, 272–3)

So began the alliance between the Church and the Crown, an alliance that would bring the Church powers that hitherto it had not possessed and that it would never possess again. It was clear that James understood that relationship of forces well enough to see that there were few areas in which he might extend his power without risking immediate confrontation. Just as the bishops began almost immediately to preach the doctrines of the divine right of kings and of non-resistance even to their wrongdoings, so the Crown found it expedient to uphold divine origin of the episcopal institution. Soon Archbishop Bancroft had marshalled enough support from the Crown to begin to eliminate Puritans from the Church. Whereas parliamentary statute required of ministers only the most general adherence to Church principles, a royal proclamation issued by James required them to adhere to every article of religion and to the officially sanctioned prayer book. Some three hundred ministers were thus purged from the Church.

James's policies as monarch and as governor of the Church provoked considerable reaction among the landowning classes, and even (a harbinger of things to come) among the mass of the population outside of the "political nation". The first few years of Charles I's reign (which began in 1625) were accordingly quite turbulent. The monarch's solution was to attempt to rule without parliament and to create an independent financial base for himself by gradually accustoming the nation to taxation by decree, and to impose upon a population whose religious beliefs and practices were ever diversifying strict uniformity of theory and practice. Charles I, even more than his father, saw the institution of the Church as being of central strategic importance not only for defending but also for extending royal authority and power. The Church in early-seventeenth-century England was in a unique position to shape public opinion and to monitor carefully political and religious discourse. In order to function as an effective ideological apparatus, however, it had to be refortified from within, purged of those clergy who would not conform to what was now a narrow set of doctrinal and ritual prescriptions or enlist themselves in the service of absolute monarchy.

The man to carry out this task was William Laud. Laud took full advantage of Charles's reliance on the Church and attempted to "restore the authority of the clergy to something like it had been in the pre-Reformation Church" (Cross 1976, 181). His reforms tended toward the shoring up of hierarchy and authority in the face of the more egalitarian practices associated with the Puritans: the rejection of Church hierarchy, including episcopacy; a minimizing of the distinction between the clergy and the lay population; a rejection of any emphasis on the visible Church, especially displays of pomp and wealth. It was clear enough to both sides in the growing conflict of the 1620s and 1630s that these notions concerning spiritual government had their secular counterparts, especially a growing sense of the absolute primacy of parliament in matters of law as well as policy. There emerged a resolute questioning of the monarchy as an institution that would reach its apogee in the late 1640s.

To counter these increasingly disturbing developments (disturbing, at least, from the point of view of the monarch and his supporters), Laud initiated a series of reforms on the authority of already existing statutes (and therefore without the approval of parliament) which cultivated in doctrine and in ritual a reverence for the mystery of authority, whether spiritual or temporal. Priests were ordered to wear the surplice, emphasizing the distinction between them and their parishioners. The communion table, which often stood in the center of the church, was ordered to be moved to the east end and railed off so as to be kept sacred. Worshippers were ordered to kneel when receiving communion and bow at the name of Jesus. The transformation of the holy table into an altar struck many clergy and lay people alike as idolatrous, just as the kneeling and bowing seemed to signify a return to pre-Reformation practices. There was a renewed emphasis on the appearance of churches: stained-glass windows were repaired, and paintings and carvings were prominently displayed. Further, Laud's reforms had the effect of limiting Charles's opponents' use of churches to mobilize and educate. Priests were enjoined to follow to the letter the service established in the Book

23

of Prayer. No one was allowed to preach a sermon until the entire service was completed. Significant numbers of both clergy and laypersons were brought before the High Commission Court for refusing to enact Laud's reforms; the ecclesiastical court was fully empowered to fine or imprison offenders.

This was without question the high point of the Church of England. As such it remained a central reference point for Swift and his High Church colleagues, an ideal that they would strive to emulate or an original moment to which they sought to return (Bennett 1975, 22). They could not see that the power of the Church during this period was not only not the norm but was in fact highly exceptional in the history of England. Further, Swift refused to accept the obvious fact, understood all too well by every monarch after 1660, that Charles I's strategic alliance with the Church had been a disastrous mistake, needlessly setting a significant part of the political nation against him. No king could afford to empower the Church as Charles I had done. Indeed, after the Restoration, the Church had constantly to defend itself from monarchs' attempts to curb its powers and extend toleration to Dissenters as a way of winning over these vital sectors of the population.

The beginning of the end came when, in 1640, Charles was forced to recall parliament for the first time in eleven years in order to raise money. After Laud had imprudently attempted to impose the Anglican Book of Prayer on the Scots a revolt had broken out. A Scottish army was marching on England and Charles needed to raise his own army, which he could not do given his limited finances. He called a parliament, which was in no mood to grant him subsidies until certain grievances in matters of Church and state were heard. The Church's own parliamentary body, the Convocation, traditionally met concurrently with parliament. However, when Charles quickly dismissed parliament (it was called the Short Parliament), the Convocation not only continued to meet, breaking tradition and seeming to suggest the independence of Church from parliament, it also passed a series of canons promoting the monarchy and the Established Church.

Charles could not forbear once again recalling parliament. Faced with war, he had little choice. This time parliament immediately set about attacking the Church. Laud was quickly impeached (and soon taken into custody) and a mass movement composed of forces that usually lay far beyond the sphere of political action pushed for a thorough reformation. A petition signed by tens of thousands called for the abolition of the Church hierarchy and its political power "Root and Branch". The institutions of the Church, its courts and its offices, were dismantled one by one, and its place in national politics permanently altered. Churches were invaded and altars and windows destroyed, and the hated railings torn down. The Anglican prayer book itself was soon outlawed. In 1644, parliament enacted "the Solemn League and Covenant" which required all clergy to swear to "endeavor the extirpation of popery, prelacy (that is church government by archbishops, bishops, their chancellors and commiseries, deans, deans and chapters, archdeacons and all other ecclesiastical officers depending on that hierarchy), superstition, heresy, schism, profaneness." Nearly one out of three clergy were ejected from their livings for refusing to swear this oath or for abetting the king (Cross 1976, 203).

In 1646, Presbyterianism was legally established as the official Church, to be governed by a council of elders elected by the congregations. But by this time the radicalization had proceeded too far for any "official" Church government really to be effective. The independents, a loose grouping of quite diverse sects, demanded individual freedom of worship and often advanced radical social demands for the abolition of all privileges of social rank and equality before the law. Parliament hesitated before the radicalism of the sects (often supported by the army), and tried, not very successfully, to preserve some form of institutional uniformity of religion as a means of social control. This fact, the indissociability of religious and social anti-authoritarianism, the inescapable tendency of religious dissent to grow into social protest in seventeenth-century England, saved the monarchy and the Church. In 1640, the majority of the ruling classes rejected absolute monarchy. Of this majority, one half sought merely to limit (to varying degrees) the power of the monarch, but viewed the abolition of monarchy, correctly, as necessarily leading to an undermining of their own authority. They understood that their political and economic power could be as well threatened from below as from above. This group viewed with growing dismay the radicalization of the years 1640–42, and ultimately sided with the king, forming the core of the Royalist camp. The other half of the landowning classes believed that it would be possible to preserve traditional social relations without the monarchy, which it regarded as destructive of its economic interests (by demanding taxes) and of its authority (through centralized government and prerogative law). This group believed that the mass mobilizations initially necessary to its power could be controlled. They ultimately pushed for the institution of a republic or commonwealth (the monarchy and the House of Lords were abolished in 1649), but found they lacked a sufficient social base on which to build the new state. In fact, an alternative to absolutism would emerge only at the end of the seventeenth century (and even then would take several decades to establish itself), the outcome of a complex of forces both national and international. In the interim, both the attempts to construct a viable absolutist state and the efforts to replace it with new state forms were condemned to failure. After 1660, a kind of absolutism manqué would have to suffice and as often as not failed to do so. In his essay *The Presbyterians Plea of Merit* (1733), Swift captured in the following way the reaction that characterized the attitudes of the ruling classes at the end of the commonwealth experiment:

> the few nobility scattered throughout the kingdom, who lived in the most retired manner, observing the confusion of things, could no longer endure to be ridden by bakers, cobblers, brewers and the like, at the head of armies; and plundering everywhere like French draggons: the Rump assembly grew despicable to those who had raised them: the city of London, exhausted by almost twenty years of contributing to their own ruin, declared against them. The rump, after many deaths and resurrections, was, in the most contemptuous manner, kicked out and burned in effigy. The excluded members were let in: a free parliament called in as legal a manner as the times would allow; and the king restored. (*Prose Works*, Vol. 12, 267–8).

The sense of a world turned upside down, of natural relations of authority not only violated but reversed ("by bakers, cobblers and brewers"), the sense not of a lapse into a Hobbesian state of nature but of a temporary, but nonetheless monstrous, suspension of the natural order of things: it was precisely this view of the English Revolution that Swift cultivated, and that he would evoke against the Whigs and the Dissenters whom he liked to regard as the descendants of the rebels.

By the end of the interregnum, the ruling classes also saw the folly of their attack on the Established Church in the concrete effects that their actions produced. Freedom of conscience in religion, that reasonable slogan, led to freedom of conscience in matters of politics and property. Similarly, legal freedom of speech seemed inescapably to lead to freedom of assembly (*de facto*, if not *de jure*). The ruling classes found that they could not grant to themselves *by law* the freedoms that they sought against the state without by that fact extending them equally to at least a significant part of the plebeian masses. Even more importantly, they found that they possessed adequate force to threaten, or even to over-throw the monarchy only by permitting and then allying with the mass mobilizations that occurred with the breakdown of civil authority, an alliance that, as Swift wrote, only "contributed to their own ruin". By 1660 they were ready to restore the Church that inculcated a sense of reverence for authority, and that dealt harshly with anyone advocating doctrinal, institutional and social innovation. Members of the ruling classes who had been sympa-thetic to Puritanism – those who remained Anglican while critical of the Laudian reforms, as well as the staunchest supporters of the Establishment – were all now ready for strict uniformity under episcopal control. Further, they wholeheartedly embraced the monarchy as the legitimate summit of the organic hierarchy that constituted society. But they supported it rather as a symbol necessary to the maintenance of social order. For the restored monarchy lacked the instruments of prerogative rule (the preroga-tive courts, forced loans and taxation by decree) that had allowed Charles I to survive without parliament. These institutional changes proved fatal to the absolutist designs first of Charles II and then James II, forcing them to rely on Louis XIV to supply the resources for building absolute rule.

Despite appearances, the relation between the Church and the monarchy would never again be what it was before 1640. Charles II learned from his father's mistakes and, however much the landed classes desired to shore up their power with an Established Church, sought to avoid polarizing the nation as his father and Laud had done a generation earlier. A cornerstone of his strategy to maintain and increase his power was the granting of general toleration in order to neutralize opposition to the monarchy on religious grounds, and perhaps to broaden his base of support. Parliament, however, in a stunning reversal of its positions of twenty years earlier, refused to hear any talk of extending tolera-tion to Presbyterians, let alone the sects. The so-called Cavalier

Parliament, elected in 1661, proceeded to pass a series of what amounted to persecutory laws. The Act of Uniformity (1662) restored and made mandatory the doctrine and rituals of the Laudian Church (including all the "idolatrous" practices that had so outraged an earlier generation). Other acts made it illegal to hold or attend any religious service that did not conform in its entirety to the prescribed forms of the Established Church. Strict censorship laws put an end to the pamphleteering that had become the hallmark of English political life. Non-conforming ministers were deprived of their livings and prevented from teaching. An abortive insurrection by the Fifth Monarchy Men only seemed to confirm their belief that dissent and disorder went hand in hand. Mandatory conformity was the order of the day, and the restored ecclesiastical courts (the most powerful of which, however, the Court of High Commission – Laud's key instrument – was never restored) did a brisk business.

As it turned out, Charles II was correct in his assessment of the balance of forces in his kingdom. He understood that the Dissenters still constituted an important part of the political nation, even if, disorganized and demoralized by the end of the interregnum, they kept quiet or masqueraded as conforming Anglicans. He knew that the very persecutory laws that were enacted to disarm and disperse non-conformists would, as before, only succeed in shaping them in the long run into an army of opposition that might pose a serious threat to his goal of ruling independently of parliament. At the same time, he realized that he could take advantage of their discontent, and offer toleration (through prerogative means) in exchange for the Dissenters' support for the prerogative power that had come to their relief (Jones 1978, 176). This led Charles to issue a Declaration of Indulgence which left the Church intact but granted rights to dissenters: the right to worship and the right to participate in political life. More menacingly, the Declaration also granted rights to Catholics, a key condition of Louis XIV's continued support for Charles's absolutist project. At the next session of parliament, Charles's action was declared illegal, his prerogative powers rejected. The Declaration was withdrawn in the face of parliament's refusal to vote Charles money. Further, parliament passed the Test Act, which forced all office holders (in civilian government at all levels, as well as the army) to take communion in the Anglican Church. Meanwhile, the Church continued its course of vigorously opposing the monarch's attempts to end or even limit the persecution of Dissenters, while simultaneously upholding as sacred the institution of the monarchy. Towards the end of his reign, however, Charles was finally forced into the alliance with the Church that he had so long avoided. In the face of increasing attacks on royal prerogative (for which dissenters who had suffered growing persecution since the Restoration furnished a mass base), he had little choice but to accept the support of the Anglican establishment and to abandon any hope of introducing toleration. His choice of William Sancroft as Archbishop of Canterbury was significant. Sancroft's program for the Church resembled Laud's in many respects (Bennett 1975, 6): he sought to strengthen the Church courts and extend Church discipline. The spontaneous political ideology of this institution was a patriarchalist theory of absolutism, and Sancroft believed that such political doctrines were indissociably part of the instruction that it was the Church's duty to provide. Thus, during the exclusion crisis of 1678–82, when there existed mass opposition to what had since the Restoration been regarded as the rightful prerogative of the king, as well as a resurgent radical republicanism, Charles had no choice but to make an alliance with the Church. The clergy preached against the sin of rebellion and warned that attacks on the monarchy were unnatural and would necessarily lead to a weakening of the bonds of authority and subjection that were necessary to social order.

When Charles II died and the Duke of York became James II, Sancroft had every reason to expect a continuation of the Church–State alliance and that, as the monarch moved towards the construction of an absolutist state, the Church, as a vital part of that state, would necessarily be strengthened. But a return to the days of Laud was not to be: there was simply no possibility of building a stable absolutist regime in the England of the 1680s. The forces that had mobilized for the exclusion of the Catholic successor, now monarch, had been defeated and persecuted in the last years of Charles's reign, but they did not disappear. The Dissenting community was highly politicized (as Charles, and soon James, saw that it would be) by the very attempts to eradicate it, and continued to furnish a permanent army of opposition united around a coherent and, by now indivisible, program of religious toleration and government by consent. The strength and determination of the opposition was briefly shown in the abortive uprising led by the Duke of Monmouth (Charles's illegitimate son, who was the Absalom of Dryden's *Absalom and Achitophel*) after the coronation of James II. Even this disreputable and discredited figure succeeded in "establishing himself in the west country and in organizing a large and effective army in a matter of two weeks" (Jones 1972, 59). Monmouth's lack of a base outside the Dissenting community led to his rapid defeat, followed by a wave of persecutions against Dissenters that only further hardened their opposition to the monarchy.

James could see that the Church, while a necessary ally at certain junctures, was ultimately an obstacle to absolute rule insofar as the exercise of its powers created a quasi-permanent opposition in whose midsts radical ideas flourished. Further, he apparently believed that only the imposition of Catholicism would decisively resolve the religious question in England (as well as bringing a much closer and more beneficial relationship with France). In order to shift the balance of forces in a direction that would favor or at least not impede his absolutist project, James issued the Declaration of Indulgence of 1687, abolishing the Test Act and all penal laws concerning non-Anglicans. When nonconformity ceased to be a crime, the very function of the Church as an ideological apparatus was called into question. Church attendance fell away and the ecclesiastical courts were nearly rendered idle. Dissenters (like the Quaker William Penn) and Catholics began to play an important and visible role in James's administration.

Thus the Anglican Church, among whose central doctrines was the divine right of kings and the sinfulness of active resistance to even their most abhorred demands, found itself under attack by the monarch that it had so assiduously defended, and finally at the center of the opposition to his absolutist project. Sancroft and the bishops hesitated before embarking on the road to opposition, hoping that James would see the error of his ways. The turning point came in 1688 when James issued an order that a second declaration, similar in content to the first, be read by all parish clergy throughout England at Sunday services. This led to the mobilization of the Church against the order and to a petition by the bishops asking that the clergy be excused from reading the declaration. Further, the petition challenged the legality of the declaration, thereby questioning the rights of the king over the Church. James's reaction was to arrest and imprison the bishops, which succeeded only in producing a mass movement for their defense. They were tried and acquitted amidst a growing sense of crisis and civil unrest, having become the focal point of the growing anti-absolutist (and anti-Catholic) mobilization.

As support for James crumbled and rumors of an invasion by William abounded, Sancroft once again asked the king to restore the Church to its rightful place, possessed of its rightful powers. Given the king's intransigence, Sancroft publicly refused his request to oppose the rumored invasion and, after the king fled, signed an order with other leading political figures calling for the navy not to oppose the Dutch and inviting William to restore order to the nation. But Sancroft refused to go any further. James II remained the monarch in the eyes of the Church, and if the Church's commitment to divine right and the ideology of patriarchalism was to have any meaning no rationalization could be allowed to justify what was essentially the overthrow of a lawful monarch. Sancroft, together with five of the seven bishops and about four hundred clergy refused to swear allegiance to William and Mary. By 1691, the non-jurors had all been deprived and while their numbers were small, "their effect on the great body of conforming Anglicans was profound: they were like a ghost of the past, confessors who stood in the ancient ways, devout, logical, insistent" (Bennett 1975, 10).

And Sancroft's effect on Swift was indeed profound. In one of his earliest extant letters (3 May 1692), Swift refers to Sancroft as "a gentleman I admire at a degree more than I can express", a sentiment more fully expressed in the "Ode to Dr. William Sancroft". Swift apparently undertook this poem, which he worked on (but never finished) between 1689 and 1692, at the behest of the Nonjuror and Jacobite former Bishop of Ely (Rosenheim, 1976). The poem, which begins with the phrase "Truth is eternal", portrays Sancroft's death as a refusal of a historical reality without alternatives. What distinguished Sancroft from many of the other Nonjurors was that he was as unwilling to support the Jacobite cause as he had been to swear allegiance to William. In some sense he recognized that absolutism in England would never again take the form of a Church–State alliance as it had under James I and Charles I, especially now that the rightful king and his heirs were Catholic. The alternative, however, was no better. Not only was William illegitimate in the eyes of the Church, but he was bent on introducing toleration, and thus reducing if not completely abolishing the temporal powers of the Church. To

31

support either monarch meant for Sancroft abandoning all the hopes he had entertained since the Restoration of a return to the "primitive" church of Hooker and Laud, doctrinally pure and with its disciplinary apparatus intact.

The "Ode to Sancroft" shows clearly that Swift, even before he formally entered the Church in 1695, saw the sweeping changes of the years immediately following the Revolution from a very determinate position, that of the Anglican institution (Rosenheim 1976). Unfortunately, nothing is known of Swift's contact with Sancroft or of his apparently extensive conversations with the former Bishop of Ely, but the "Ode" exhibits the profound sense of fear and disgust that many of the clergy shared in the face of what was felt to be an all-out attack on the Church. England has become a "a dwelling place to fiends" where "sin and plague ever abound". William, the "too gentle King", is surrounded by "a thousand poisonous weeds" which threaten to "overshade the royal rose". The "weathercock of state" is "hung loosely on the church's pinnacle", but the "herd beneath" thinks that the Church must turn with the State. They do not understand that the Church expresses an eternal and immutable order, which is in turn the necessary foundation of any state. The efforts of the "wild reformers" of "this outcast age" will only destroy the Church: "religion now does on her deathbed lie".

What were the reforms before which the "primitive Sancroft" faded? The Toleration Act of 1689 abolished mandatory conformity for the general population and allowed Dissenters to worship separately in their own meeting houses. During the first year after the Act, over a thousand licensed and unlicensed meeting-houses were established (Bennett 1975, 13). While the attendance at some churches was still required by law, the practical effects of the Act were to loosen the hold of religion in general. Attendance at Anglican services declined drastically and steadily. Dissenting academies, their legal status unclear, multiplied throughout the nation. While the Test Act remained in force, the legalization of dissent encouraged the practice of occasional conformity. The Church courts, which still possessed the power to impose the penalty of excommunication, were often prevented by severe financial limitations from pursuing even the most egregious cases. Even more disturbing was the fact that excommunications were routinely annulled en masse by parliament. Further, the bishops appointed to take the place of the Nonjurors tended, as might be expected, to be sympathetic to the Whigs and, in general, to favor toleration. The lower clergy quickly came to see their own episcopate as in league with the enemies of the Church.

In 1695, the Licensing Act, which had given the Church hierarchy the power to censor theological works, expired: "heresy and attacks on the ministers of God now became virtually unpunishable, and a flood of heterodox and anti-clerical literature poured on to the popular bookmarket" (Bennett 1975, 19). Not only was the disciplinary power of the Church severely reduced, but it had to contend with an ideological assault that submitted even the most sacred doctrines to scathing criticism. The clergy had mobilized against James in 1688 because it was believed that the very existence of the Church was at stake. With the exception of the Nonjurors (who themselves, as we have seen, opposed James), they greeted the new order with relief and regarded the Revolution settlement as an effective safeguard of the Church's legal existence. The assault on the Church's monopoly of religious life that immediately followed provoked a renewed mobilization of the lower clergy, who saw the king, his increasingly Whig ministers and the episcopal bench as a combined threat to the natural order of things. Many of the younger leaders whose actions had helped usher in the Revolution turned against, if not the Revolution itself, some of its most essential effects. "The Church in Danger" became the rallying cry of the Church party for an entire generation.

However, given the momentous changes that were rapidly transforming England's economy into the most advanced in the world, the changes in the institution of the Church and its place in society seem minimal in comparison. Locke's plea for toleration (which would have converted the Anglican Church into a purely voluntary association with no legal privileges) as an essential characteristic of a truly free and prosperous commonwealth went unheard, even as the capitalist development to which religious freedom would seem to correspond continued to accelerate. There is no doubt that powerful "modernizing" tendencies existed (of which Locke was only one, and by no means the most radical, expression) and carried on a permanent offensive against the privileges of the Church. But they never entirely succeeded: the Church survived amidst unprecedented and unforeseeable historical change, possessed of a decelerating temporality detached from and running counter to the accelerating temporalities of the divergent institutions and practices that surrounded it. The survival of the

Church was an effect of the complexity and conflict proper to the bourgeois revolution in England.

The war with France that began shortly after William came to power and lasted, with a brief intermission, for the next twenty years, was initially an effect of capitalist development only to become one of its most powerful causes. English commercial interests demanded a more aggressive foreign policy to protect, and later to further, their role in the New World, Africa and the Mediterranean. With the growth of French economic power, Dutch interests coincided with the English. Thus William, with the approbation of key commercial and financial concerns, undertook the most expensive war in English history. Its effects on English society, as Swift was later to write in his most successful work of propaganda, *The Conduct of the Allies*, were manifold. It brought into being economic institutions whose size and complexity dazzled contemporary observers: the Bank of England, the stock market, joint-stock companies. The war also brought into being deficit spending and government debt, together with seemingly numberless opportunities for speculation. These financial innovations in turn permitted a massive growth of the state. The size of the navy doubled between 1689 and 1697 (Plumb 1967, 119). The army grew at an even greater rate and, in contrast to earlier times, became a permanent feature of the modern state. At the same time the financial apparatus of the state expanded to keep pace with trade, especially the departments concerned with customs, excise and taxation. The importance and centrality of the court diminished in relation to these departments and sub-departments of state. Finally, the land tax was introduced to provide a stable source of revenue.

However, the spectacular growth of the economy and the state produced inescapable contradictions. Throughout the 1690s and into the first decades of the eighteenth century a process of differentiation occurred, separating the landowning classes into a significant minority who benefited from the economic changes and were able to establish commercial and financial roots, and those whose economic position was weakened often because their wealth was concentrated exclusively in land, which left them disproportionately burdened by the land tax and falling prices. The latter were initially Whigs who had resented James's intrusion in what they considered their jurisdiction, the realms in which they were – as the most prominent, or at least among the most prominent, landlords of their county – the "natural authorities" among tenants and small farmers. By the end of William's reign a coalition of opposition began to take shape, uniting discontented landowners with parish clergy in a country party (at first divided among Whigs and Tories, but soon identified with the new Tory Party of Harley and St John (soon to be Lord Bolingbroke) dedicated to the defense or revivification of "the old England".

It was this alliance that, together with the accession of Queen Anne, "the last Stuart", who was known to be devoted to the Church of England, gave new hope to the Church party. Their first counterattack came in the form of a parliamentary campaign against occasional conformity, an issue on which, as the clergy saw it, the fate of the "primitive church" depended. It increasingly appeared that the Anglican Church was the Established Church in name only, its legal privileges merely fictions. To outlaw occasional conformity was to restore to the church its proper power and to begin to agitate (it was hoped, with the support of the queen) "for a return to the past when Church and State had conjoined in a single authoritarian regime" (Bennett 1975, 22). At the same time, the Tory squirearchy saw the outlawing of occasional conformity as a way of shifting the balance of forces in parliament and the state in their favor. The Whigs depended on urban Dissenters for much of their grassroots organizing and campaigning (Jones 1978, 323). An Occasional Conformity bill would have disrupted the system of patronage upon which such networks depended by excluding Dissenters from even local offices. The passage of such a bill would have driven a significant number of Whigs out of politics. While such bills passed the House of Commons, they were consistently defeated in the Whig-dominated House of Lords. During this same period the lower clergy began actively mobilizing for more power within the Church in order to carry out a revanchist political program that the more moderate Bishops (most of whom had been appointed by William III, after the departure of the Nonjurors) resisted. Their militancy, however, disturbed the queen, who saw the attacks of the lower clergy on their ecclesiastical superiors as subversive of the proper relations of hierarchy and subordination in Church and State. The elections of 1705 produced a solid Whig majority and the High Church Party was forced into retreat.

Swift's position during these important developments was characteristically contradictory. Perhaps because the Test Act had not yet been extended to Ireland (it was not until 1704 that the Test was applied as part of the anti-Catholic legislation of the period), Swift (who was in England at the time), at least as he expresses himself in his correspondence at the end of 1703, seems confused by the heated debates over occasional conformity, unable to grasp what is at stake. Although he acknowledges that "the whole body of the clergy, with a great majority of Commons were violent for this bill", he declares himself "much at a loss" (1963, Vol. 1, 39). The Whig leadership, in whose favor he has been since the publication of *Contests and Dissensions* in 1701 have assured him that rejecting the Bill to outlaw occasional conformity will not "hurt the Church or do kindness to the Dissenters"(39). Three months later Swift reports that he has written against the bill, but that his efforts arrived too late from the printer and therefore were never circulated (44). He has indeed moved far from the positions expressed in the "Ode to Sancroft": there is no sense of the Church in danger and he is willing to oppose the "whole body of the clergy" and defend the right of Dissenters to participate in political life by taking communion once a year. This is indeed a "kindness to Dissenters", probably a tactical concession to the Whig lords in whom Swift still placed his political confidence. But, despite his demonstrations of loyalty, his "patrons" never returned the favor. And for good reason: Swift's *A Tale of a Tub*, published the same year, ferociously attacked the Dissenters and ridiculed even the most moderate of their criticisms of the Anglican Church (Harth 1961).

For the next several years, the Whigs, emboldened by their electoral success, launched an offensive against the Church, attempting to weaken it financially and militating for a repeal of the Test. When Swift arrived in England in 1707 seeking the remission of the tax paid by the Irish clergy to the Crown (the First Fruit and Twentieth Parts), he found the Whig leadership willing to support such a measure only if the Test were repealed in Ireland, which they viewed as a prelude to its repeal at home. (It was in response to this suggestion that Swift wrote *An Argument Against Abolishing Christianity* in 1708.)

The emergence of a clear anti-clerical platform among the Whigs soon alienated the queen who, along with the lower clergy, increasingly looked to the reign of her grandfather and great-grandfather (Charles I and James I) for political and ecclesiastical inspiration. As soon as it was felt that the alliance between the queen and the High Church Party was secure, and that she had finally turned her back on the Whigs and everything they stood for, the clergy quickly reversed the entire emphasis of their propaganda. Whereas since 1689 the Church had defended its independence from the state and the Crown by appealing to medieval statute and custom, by 1709 the possibility of a renewed alliance between Church and State, the likes of which had not been seen since before James II, stimulated renewed interest in theories of divine right and passive obedience. In this sense, the marked shift in doctrine as well as in tone that separates Swift's *The Sentiments of a Church of England Man*, written in 1708, from the *Examiner* essays of 1710–11 is typical of the time. The alignment of social forces that characterized the conjuncture thus permitted the revival of authoritarian and even absolutist ideas, together with the hope that they might actually be realized. Since 1706, when the French were driven out of Italy and the Spanish Netherlands, there was an increasing sense that the war was continuing only for the sake of the financial interests that stood directly to benefit from it. Nearly twenty years of war had produced a mass opposition to Whig rule and to the values associated with it.

In reaction to the secularizing efforts of the Whigs, the High Church Party, with the full backing of its country allies and the queen, began to project its own program: an infusion of financial support that would allow the restoration of decaying Church properties and the building of new churches, a strengthening of the ecclesiastical courts and of the entire disciplinary machinery of the Church, and the vigorous suppression of all forms of dissent and heresy. Mass support for this program crystallized around the trial of a High Church zealot, Henry Sacheverell, at the hands of the Whig ministry. In 1709, Sacheverell had preached a sermon at the invitation of the City Corporation in which he both excoriated Dissenters and Anglican advocates of toleration and advanced openly absolutist (but not Jacobite) theories. Because he indirectly attacked Whig leaders, he was charged with seditious libel. Although he was found guilty, his judges, intimidated by widespread pro-Church sentiment (the most palpable manifestations of which were the daily demonstrations outside Westminster Hall), saw fit to pass only the lightest of sentences. Tory leaders immediately sent Sacheverell on a "victory tour" around the country, mobilizing support for the next round of parliamentary elections. The High Church Party enjoyed greater popular support than at any time since its mobilization against James II twenty years earlier. With a mass base and solid backing among the landed classes, the party prepared an offensive. Its chief propagandist was Jonathan Swift.

The elections of 1710 produced a large Tory majority, marking the beginning of that period, "the last four years of the Queen's ministry", in which not only Swift's politics but those of an entire generation were defined. It was believed that the time had finally come to restore the natural authority of landlord over tenant and priest over parishioner, all presided over by a benevolent sovereign increasingly possessed of her rightful prerogative powers: a fixed and immutable social hierarchy. No longer limited by the need for compromise, the way was opened for the more extreme elements in the Tory Party (who soon formed the "October Club") to launch a campaign of political and religious persecution, with the aim of creating "a single party in church and state" to make possible such a restoration. In 1711, occasional conformity was legally banned. Two years later the Schism Act reinforced the Anglican monopoly on education by declaring that only those who conformed to the Church of England would be allowed to establish or run any school, public or private. At the same time, the Qualification Act of 1710 imposed substantial property qualifications on all MPs, thereby excluding "townsmen, most of whose wealth was in joint-stock and working capital, not landed property." (Jones 1978, 38).

However, just as the war determined the rise of the High Church Party and its Tory allies – insofar as they rode the wave of war-weariness and articulated the demands of all the victims, high and low, of Britain's unprecedented economic progress – so the war and the commercial expansion of which it was the expression brought them to an insurmountable and irreversible crisis that finally pushed the Tories out of power for the next fifty years. The question of how precisely to end the war, and on what conditions, exposed the internal contradictions of Toryism. For, despite the fact that a majority of the landed classes had mobilized against the specific form of financing the war, the land tax, they generally recognized that their own economic advantage lay in ensuring Britain's commercial predominance, which was exactly what was at stake in the conflict with France. This was a fact recognized by later Whig regimes, especially that of Robert Walpole who deliberately kept the land tax at a minimum in order to deprive the opposition of a sufficiently activist base. A majority of the Tories, however they might rail at the new England, were inextricably bound up with it. They tended to take the whole for its parts; but when specific grievances, like the land tax, were addressed their ardor cooled. Similarly, they might denounce the ever-expanding bureaucracy, the standing professional army, and the new modes of finance, but most Tories never seriously sought to reverse these developments. Many, without the pressure of the war, stood to benefit from them. A minority – albeit a significant minority in which were included many of the key Tory leaders and propagandists – embraced, or at least considered embracing, eighteenth-century Britain's politics of despair: Jacobitism.

The issue that finally developed the contradictions of the Tory project was the question of the succession. Those who mobilized against the abuses of the system (excessive taxation, financial corruption, prolonged military interventions), but who consciously or unconsciously accepted it, acquiesced in the Hanoverian succession, even if the Hanoverians were likely to favor the Whigs. To a majority of Tories, the alternative, a Stuart Restoration, was unthinkable; it meant absolutism in the French manner and the imposition of Catholicism. It also meant a return to the past, a reversal of the major economic and political developments since 1689. And this was precisely the allure of Jacobitism to an increasingly alienated minority, especially after the collapse of the Tory Party in 1714 with the death of the queen. They came to see that the party did not simply, as was so often asserted, founder on the quarrel between its two principal leaders, Harley and Bolingbroke. This quarrel was itself symptomatic of the split between those who accepted the "new England" and those who did not and yearned for a return to some indeterminate past. By 1714, the contradiction had grown even more acute. The key legislative reforms of which the Tories had been so proud proved unenforceable from the start. Dissenters continued to masquerade as conforming Anglicans to gain office or place, and dissenting academies never stopped turning out pupils. Similarly, the land qualification was easily circumvented by city merchants and financiers. Most Tories grudgingly accepted *de facto* toleration and the presence of the monied men in the political world. But others, among them a disproportionate number of clergy, were pushed toward ideological extremism, toward a wholesale rejection of actually existing British society. They had awakened to the passage of time, that is, historical development, to see an unceasing movement away from what was felt to be the eternal and immutable order of things. The political and religious themes around which the party had mobilized mass support (the defense of the Church of England, a return to natural authority and tradition) were gradually deprived of their urgency and importance, and the ideological underpinnings of these themes began to take on an archaic air. The clergy, who once thought of themselves as the guardians of a newly restored order, were left to accept the merely *de jure* or nominal character of their institution, which survived as a decorative feature of a heteroclite state in a rapidly developing capitalist economy. The mere survival of the Church, together with lower taxes and a growing economy, were enough to placate the squirearchy and induce them to suffer the post-1714 order. Whatever concessions the Whig leadership made were well worth the outcome.

For Swift, and for an entire generation of clergy, the disintegration of the Tory Party meant an end to all their hopes of an ecclesiastical restoration. The recognition, so long deferred, of the Church's irreversible decline was now inescapable. It was a time of ideological crisis and political pessimism. The Whigs, with the full support of George I, quickly repealed the pro-Church legislation of the queen's last ministry, suppressed the Convocation, and nullified all the exclusionary effects of the Test without repealing the act itself. The king, upon assuming the throne, issued a decree barring clergy from delivering sermons on political topics. Whig divines like Benjamin Hoadly argued the absolute authority of parliament over the Church. Further, the Whigs carried out an extensive purge of Tories and passed the Septennial Act, extending the time between parliamentary elections to seven years. The possibility of Tories appealing to their mass base was significantly undercut by the passage of the Riot Act, which banned assemblies of more than twelve people whose purpose was criticism of the government. While these developments had the effect of driving some Tories (including most of Swift's closest associates) into the Jacobite camp, the Whigs had correctly calculated that the primary result of their offensive would be the demoralization and dispersal of the opposition. When the Pretender invaded Scotland in 1715, hoping to spark an uprising, few Tories responded. At the same time, a united Tory opposition in parliament would not take shape until 1725. It was in this interval, from his bitter "exile" in Ireland, that Swift wrote *Gulliver's Travels*.

Thus Swift, like all high Anglicans, came finally to recognize that the state necessary to empower the Church once again and restore to it its just and proper functions was an impossibility. The refusal of certain of his colleagues to accept the historical impasse that the Church faced led them to the utter futility of Jacobitism (without the slightest guarantee that the Catholic Pretender would not simply repeat his father's attempt to restore the Roman Church to England). In contrast, Swift seems to flee into the imaginary solution: a vision of Church and State, an ideal that could not be described in expository form but only figured negatively in literary satire. From now on, in the ideological realm, it was less and less possible to state the Anglican philosophy; instead one had to learn how to be an Anglican *in* philosophy, to occupy positions that, no matter how foreign to traditional Anglican thought, objectively favored the interests of the Church, if only by weakening its enemies. It was in this way that Swift came to enter the prolonged battle of the books.

2

A Perpetual War:
To Be an Anglican
in Philosophy

And truly when I compare the former enemies to Christianity, such
as Socinus, Hobbes and Spinosa; with such of their successors, as
Toland, Asgil, Coward, Gildon, this author of the *Rights*, and some
others; the Church appeareth to me like the sick old lion in the
fable, who after having his person outraged by the Bull, the
Elephant, the Horse, and the Bear, took nothing so much to heart,
as to find himself at last insulted by the Spurn of an Ass.

SWIFT, "Remarks upon a Book, Intitled,
The Rights of the Christian Church"

Swift shared with a number of the most important Anglican
thinkers of the late seventeenth century the notion that the history
of ideas had been one long *combat des livres*, a notion that explains
why he was as fiercely partisan in philosophy as in politics. It is
no accident that both Swift and Atterbury, two of the most important propagandists for the High Church Party in the first quarter
of the eighteenth century, should first gain experience in what
appears today to be an uninteresting, if not embarrassing, debate
concerning the relative merits of the Ancients and the Moderns.
Swift and Atterbury were, of course, on the losing side, or rather
the side that appeared at the time to have triumphed through the
literary and rhetorical skill of the partisans of the Ancients but
whose leading minds, the superannuated Sir William Temple and
the jejune Charles Boyle, posed no threat to the progress of scholarship (and proved no match for the intrepid Richard Bentley).[1] But
Swift's *Battle of the Books*, which was published with *A Tale of a Tub*,
is not simply an intervention in a specific debate: it can also be

seen as a presentation of the history of philosophy as perpetual war (Montag 1989), which would thus justify Swift's *parti pris*. At stake in the conflicts that traversed the history of ideas were, as Swift announced in one of the pieces prefatory to *A Tale*, the very foundations of "religion and government" (*Prose Works*, Vol. 1, 24).[2]

To speak of seventeenth-century philosophy as perpetual war, however, is to risk a paradox: for did not this philosophy even in its diversity seek precisely to put an end to the conflict of opinions that preceded it by bringing to bear an axiomatic discourse whose necessary truth would be guaranteed by its resemblance to the operations of geometry? If we take the word of seventeenth-century philosophy itself – or at least that which is now presented as seventeenth-century philosophy – its essence conforms to its appearance: that of an untroubled order of reasons which put an end to controversy. However, as Alexandre Koyré has noted, the history of seventeenth-century thought was written by those who emerged victorious from its struggles (1965, 62). Defeated theoretical positions are regarded as mere survivals of earlier philosophies (for example, Platonism and Scholasticism) or simply vanish into the abyss of "error" (Althusser 1976, 142–50). The admittedly marginal discourses of Anglican philosophers like Ralph Cudworth, Henry More, and Richard Bentley are in fact difficult to delineate in a precise way; they are often not clearly demarcated from the philosophies they claim to oppose. The Anglican opponents of Descartes, Hobbes and Spinoza are often charged with eclecticism and incoherence. The ragged prolixity of Cudworth (whose *True Intellectual System of the Universe* comes to nearly two thousand pages) stands in stark contrast to the economy of the *Meditations* or the crystalline structure of Spinoza's *Ethics*, even more as Cudworth seeks to demonstrate the existence of an Aristotelian world-view in which Descartes has his proper (if subordinate) place. We would be mistaken, however, if we failed to see that this eclecticism, the coupling of incompatible and opposing doctrines, constitutes a position itself, the very prolixity of the "demonstration" being a sign of its defensive and hopeless character. This eclecticism opens up a space (or provides a vantage point) from which we may see an image of seventeenth-century thought very different from the image that the age succeeded in transmitting to us. From this space we do not see a sweeping away of error followed by the orderly progress of reason. Rather, we see nothing less than a war.

Even the most moderate of the Anglican thinkers, those most sympathetic to the scientific discoveries of the seventeenth century and the discontinuities they introduced into philosophical reflection, were forced to abandon the promise of perpetual peace offered by both the empiricisms and the rationalisms of the time and to fall back on the Platonic conception of philosophy as "perpetual war". Cudworth (probably the most capable of the Cambridge Platonists and once the tutor of Swift's erstwhile patron, Sir William Temple) saw the philosophical scene of his time as a confirmation of Plato's argument in *The Sophist*

> that there had always been, as well as then there was, a perpetual war and controversy in the world and as he calls it a kind of gigantomachy betwixt these two parties or sects of men; the one, that held that there was no other substance in the world besides body; the other that asserted incorporeal substance. (Cudworth 1845, Vol. 1, 35)

By the end of the century the very philosophers who explicitly sought to put an end to philosophical controversy were often regarded as carrying on the conflict they seemed to denounce, if in a more subtle form. Even the prudent Descartes seemed to carry on the war in the guise of peace. His professed intentions, his defense of incorporeal substance against the likes of Hobbes, seemed in contradiction to the actual theoretical effects of his work. Henry More had initially greeted the Cartesian system with alacrity, hailing it as the antidote to Hobbes's atheism, only to draw back in horror at the realization that Descartes' defense of incorporeal substance was simply a maneuver designed to outflank and confuse his critics (Koyré 1957, 110–24; Cudworth 1845, Vol. 1, 105–6).

Cudworth and More were thus forced to reflect not only upon the content of the philosophical war but upon its form, the strategies and even tactics employed by the partisans of matter in their attack on the camp of spirit. The task of describing the war and its major encounters was made infinitely more difficult by the fact that the partisans of matter, instead of openly avowing their adversarial position, chose to declare themselves allies of those they hoped to overthrow. Disguise and impersonation were among the most effective tactics:

> as Epicurus, so other Atheists in like manner have commonly had their vizards and disguises; Atheism for the most part prudently choosing to walk about in masquerade. And though some over credulous persons

have been so far imposed upon hereby to conclude that there was hardly any such thing as an Atheist anywhere in the world, yet they that are sagacious may easily look through those thin veils and disguises and perceive these Atheists oftentimes insinuating their Atheism even then, when they most of all profess themselves theists. (Cudworth 1845, Vol. 1, 105–6)

From its origins philosophy had been a struggle between systems that Cudworth named after their greatest champions: the "Aristotelical" and the "Democritical" (ibid., 94–5). The Aristotelical system was to be sure not a codification of the Aristotelian corpus, nor was it identical to the crumbling edifice of Scholasticism, itself based on Thomas Aquinas's reading of Aristotle. Rather, for Cudworth (and for Swift, as will be seen), the Aristotelical denoted a conceptual apparatus that was designed to serve with equal facility religious, scientific and political ends. It was an Aristotelianism peculiar to Anglican thought, an Aristotelianism shorn of scholastic superfluities and which knew enough to be silent on the scientific matters that the scholastics were imprudent enough to discuss. It proved to be a fairly flexible instrument, designed to incorporate new forms of knowledge as well as to accommodate social and political changes without having to alter its fundamental and essential tenets. The necessary components of the system were enumerated in Book I of Richard Hooker's *Of the Laws of Ecclesiastical Polity*. Hooker described a world ruled by laws, defining natural law as "that which God hath decreed". The world was ruled by divine commandment: "all things that are have some operations not violent or causal. Neither doth anything ever begin to exercise the same without some foreconceived end for which it worketh" (1969, Vol. 1, 150). The world was permanently ordered and the hierarchical disposition of its parts enforced by final, noncorporeal causes. Such a concept of natural law, however, contained an ambiguity: the law was both the designation of an end or purpose and a commandment to fulfill that purpose. It thus offered "the ambiguity of constraint and ideal" (Althusser 1972, 32). Hooker writes:

For we see the whole world and each part thereof so compacted that as long as each thing performeth only that work which is natural to it, it thereby preserveth both other things and also itself. Contrariwise, let any principal thing such as the sun, the moon, any one of the elements or heavens, but once cease or fail or swerve and who doth not easily conceive that the sequel thereof would be ruin to itself and

whatsoever dependeth on it. And it is possible that man being not only
the noblest creature in the world but even a very world in himself, his
transgressing the law of his nature should draw no manner of harm
after it? (1969, Vol. 1, 185–6)

Hooker's conception of natural law allowed for the possibility
of its transgression by man (Cudworth 1845, Vol. 1, 94–5).
Cudworth regarded the Democritical system as the philosophical
justification of this transgression. By positing a universe ruled only
by material and efficient causes, consisting only of matter (whatever its specific form) in motion without either foundation or
ultimate end, the Democritical philosophers ruled out the idea of
a natural society, a state proper to human nature. The opposition
of Aristotle and Democritus was thus for Cudworth an opposition
proper to philosophy, a conflict that came into the world with
philosophy (the pre-Socratics) and from which it seemed doomed
never to free itself. And the Anglican thinkers were not alone in
thinking so. Their adversaries, most of whom, it is true, avoided
saying so in public, tended to share this reading of the history of
philosophy. The name Aristotle had become a conceptual linchpin connecting a number of quite diverse philosophical and religious notions and was thus, according to a writer's philosophical
allegiances, either an insuperable obstacle to the development of
knowledge or a bulwark against intellectual and ultimately political anarchy.

We may understand the vehemence of Cudworth's defense of
Aristotelian philosophy (the particulars of which he found it expe-
dient to dispense with) in his *True Intellectual System of the Universe*
when we set it in relation to the work of Descartes, Hobbes,
Gassendi and Spinoza and their offensive against the ruling ideas.
In the preface to the French edition of *Principles of Philosophy* (1644),
Descartes wrote that of the ancient philosophers

> the first and principal whose writings we possess are Plato and Aristo-
> tle, between whom the only difference that exists is that the former
> following the steps of his master Socrates, ingenuously confessed that
> he had never been able to discover anything for certain and was con-
> tent to set down the things that seemed to him to be probable, for this
> end adopting certain principles whereby he tried to account for other
> things. Aristotle, on the other hand, had less candour and although he
> had been Plato's disciple for twenty years and possessed no other prin-
> ciples than his master's, he entirely changed the method of stating them

and proposed them as true and certain although there was no appearance of his ever having held them to be such. (1985, Vol. 1, 181)

Descartes thus offered an explanation for the failure of Aristotelian philosophy and science. Not only did Aristotle lack a method for discovering truths of indisputable certainty; even more, he denied this very lack (the acknowledgement of which had been the great virtue of Socratic and Platonic inquiry). In contrast, Hobbes, in a passage from the *Leviathan* that earned him infamy in his own time, left to the side particular disputes with Aristotle and the School in favor of general invective: "there is nothing so absurdly said in natural philosophy than that which is now called Aristotle's *Metaphysics*; nor more repugnant to government than much of what he hath said in his politics; nor more ignorantly than a great part of his *Ethics*" (1968, 687).

At the same time, Aristotle was not simply a metonym for the whole of ancient thought. The attack on his philosophy was not a dismissal of ancient thought, as is often argued, but rather constituted an integral part of a process by which the hierarchy of its doctrines was retroactively reordered. Plato, for example, received qualified praise from both Descartes and Hobbes because of the importance accorded mathematics in Platonic thought (Descartes 1985, Vol. 1, 181; Hobbes 1968, 686). But even more highly valued was the tradition of ancient atomism. "Democritus", wrote Hobbes, "taught me what was silly and how much more one man knows than the crowd" (Hobbes 1679, 4; Sarasohn 1985, 363–79). Gassendi began his philosophical career with an attack on the scholastic dialectic in the *Exercises Against the Aristotelians* (1624), but achieved notoriety for his role in the rehabilitation of atomism. His *De Vita et Doctrina Epicuri* demonstrated that Epicurean philosophy was a distant and nearly forgotten foreshadowing of the truths of modern science as well as of the methods by which they might be discovered. Finally, Spinoza, in response to a correspondent who had invoked Plato and Aristotle in support of an argument for the existence of spirits and ghosts, stated that

the authority of Plato, Aristotle and Socrates does not carry much weight with me. I should have been astonished, if you had brought forward Epicurus, Democritus, Lucretius, or any of the atomists or upholders of the atomic theory. It is no wonder that persons who have invented occult qualities, intentional species, substantial forms and a thousand other trifles should have also devised spectres and ghosts and

47

given credence to old wives' tales in order to take away the reputation of Democritus whom they were so jealous of that they burnt all the books he had published amid so much eulogy. (Wolf 1966, 290)

The valorization of atomism was more alluded to than explained by the great philosophers of the age. The nearly silent reordering and redistribution of the history of philosophy thus took place at the margins of the theoretical transformations of the seventeenth century. The question of historical filiation was vastly overshadowed by the major philosophers' attempts to dissociate themselves from the dominant tradition and to declare in clear and distinct terms the radical novelty of their endeavors. The question of historical filiation, however, did not escape the informed gaze of Cudworth, who contested the disavowal of history characteristic of the new philosophers. He sought to disprove the claim that contemporary philosophical reasoning was truly new and thus separated by a gulf from earlier traditions. He began by developing the marginal admissions of these thinkers to describe in detail the historical filiations that bound their philosophy to certain ancient traditions. In his hands, the history of philosophy seemed less a progression than a series of recurrences, an indefinite but inescapable repetition of that "gigantomachy" between the partisans of matter and the partisans of spirit. Thus Cudworth could argue that, because Descartes and Hobbes simply defended positions already demarcated by such pre-Socratics as Democritus and Leucippus, Aristotle, having refuted the ancient materialists, had in a sense refuted their modern followers *avant la lettre*. Of course, Aristotle did not simply deny or negate atomistic doctrines but rather restored certain of them to their proper (subordinate and limited) place in the theoretical framework that his philosophy provided.

> The whole Aristotelical system of thought is infinitely to be preferred before the whole of the Democritical; though the former hath been so much disparaged and the other cried up among us. Because though it cannot be denied but that the Democritical hypothesis doth much more handsomely and intelligibly resolve the corporeal phenomena yet in all those other things, which are the greatest moment, it is rather a madness than a philosophy. But the Aristotelic system is right and sound as to those greater things: in asserting incorporeal substance, a deity distinct from the world, the naturality of morality and liberty of will. (Cudworth 1845, Vol. 1, 94–5)

The "greater things" of which the Aristotelic system, according to Cudworth, was the most perfect expression, are precisely the themes over which Swift's *A Tale of a Tub* broods obsessively, and to which it persistently returns in the disorder of its unfolding by means of a dazzling array of rhetorical devices. The *Tale* never strays far from these nodal points, through which every one of its diverse threads seems to pass. Swift's most definitive statement on the Aristotelical system and its place in the history of thought, however, appears in Book Three of *Gulliver's Travels*. Although written some twenty years after *A Tale*, it exhibits a curious (and, in *Gulliver's Travels*, anomalous) recollection of the battle of the books in which Swift had participated, a battle all but forgotten by 1726. On the island of Glubbdubdrib, Gulliver is given the power "to call up whatever numbers among all the dead from the beginning of the world to the present time and command them to answer any question he should think fit to ask" (*Prose Works* Vol. II, 179). Gulliver accordingly proposes that Aristotle appear at the head of his commentators and finds that Aristotle

> was all out of patience with the account I gave him of Scotus and Ramus as I presented them to him…. I then desired the governor to call up Descartes and Gassendi with whom I prevailed to explain their systems to Aristotle. This great philosopher freely acknowledged his own mistakes in natural philosophy, because he proceeded in many things upon conjecture as all men must do; and he found that Gassendi, who had made the doctrines of Epicurus as palatable as he could, and the vortices of Descartes equally exploded. He predicted the same fate for attraction whereof the present learned are such zealous asserters. He said that new systems were but new fashions, which would vary in every age; and even those who pretend to demonstrate them from mathematical principles would flourish but a short period of time and be out of vogue when that was determined. (*Prose Works* Vol. II, 181–2)

Swift's defense of Aristotle converges with that of Cudworth in its essentials: both, when examined, allude to a profound philosophical crisis which had matured considerably in the interval that separated *Gulliver's Travels* (1726) from *The True Intellectual System* (1678). Symptomatic of the crisis were Cudworth's significant concessions to Democritical philosophy, specifically its atomistic and Cartesian variants. The "essentials" of the Aristotelical system (final causes, incorporeal substance, the naturality of law) constituted a mere skeleton and were, if anything, increasingly foreign to the body of propositions that they, in their ensemble, supposedly upheld. The critique of materialism, while still carried out in the name of Aristotle, came to be a critique internal to materialism itself. Thus Cudworth argues that atomism "(rightly understood) affordeth no manner of shelter or protection to [atheism]" but is "the greatest bulwark and defence against the same" (1845, Vol. 1, xi). Further, Cudworth even turned Descartes' philosophy against itself, attacking certain of its propositions under the standard of "clear and distinct ideas" (275).

By the end of the seventeenth century, the Anglican intelligentsia had abandoned so many of their long-held positions in order to engage the enemy on his own terrain that their philosophy became virtually indistinguishable from that which they claimed to oppose. The Boyle lectureship, established in 1691 by Robert Boyle, provided a platform for liberal Anglican thinkers to attack what were felt to be the atheistic implications of the new philosophy and science (Jacobs 1976, 143–200). The inaugural lectures were delivered by none other than Richard Bentley, whose subject was "The Folly and Unreasonableness of Atheism". These lectures marked the virtual disappearance of Aristotelian teleology into the well-ordered universe described by Newton (in conjunction with whom Bentley prepared the lectures) (Koyré 1957, 179). Going considerably further than either Cudworth or More, Bentley's antidote to atheism was nothing less than a good dose of atheism itself. He sought to turn "all the batteries and towers that the Atheists have raised against heaven" against the atheists themselves (Vol. 3, 75). All references to Aristotle vanished. The doctrines that had once possessed a decidedly subordinate place in the Aristotelian framework came to supplant that framework itself. Bentley hailed the recent rediscovery of ancient materialism: "the mechanical or corpuscular philosophy, though peradventure, the oldest as well as the best in the world, had lain buried for many ages in contempt and oblivion, till it was happily restored and cultivated by some excellent wits of the present age" (Vol. 3, 74). He went on to argue that mechanical or corpuscular philosophy is "friendly ... to the immateriality of human souls, and consequently to the existence of a supreme being" (Vol. 3, 74). No longer could the order of the world be inferred from the existence of God; rather, the existence of God must itself be inferred from the regularity of the laws governing the natural world.

It is in relation to the retreat of Anglican philosophy that Swift's peculiar defense of Aristotle must be understood. Anglican Aristotelianism had all but disappeared, its positions and fortifications having been abandoned as too weak and unprotected. The *Tale* and, later, *Gulliver's Travels* emerge as a final testimony to this crisis and is therefore a defense of the indefensible, of doctrines that had become untenable and even unthinkable. The philosophical positions that they invoke could no longer be formulated in an analytic or synthetic chain of propositions; indeed, they could not even be formulated as declarative utterances. It remains the task of analysis to uncover not hidden meanings, intentions or influences in the work but rather the indelible traces of the despairing silence upon which it is built, the unstateable theses whose absence renders the work hollow and incomplete. What are the statements to which the work, often without acknowledgement, refers and which, in their ensemble, form its conditions of possibility? What are the truths, unthinkable by Swift's time, that *A Tale* and *Gulliver's Travels* defend but often cannot name, the truths for which there is no longer room in a full, teeming world?

Let us begin with *A Tale of a Tub*. Henceforth, Swift's ideological struggle could be waged only from behind enemy lines, no longer *in propria persona* but solely by means of parody and impersonation. The disorder of *A Tale* is neither simply an absence of order (and therefore a literary fault) nor a parody of disorder (which would presuppose, for the work to be intelligible, a unified intention or a hidden structure). The cause of the work is neither to be found in Swift's intention nor in the necessity of form, but in a group of conflicts that traverse the heterogeneous discursive field that is philosophy at the close of the seventeenth century. Three conflicts in particular emerge as nodal points or themes within *A Tale*: (i) the madness of method; (ii) the problematization of spirit; (iii) language as matter.[3]

I. The Madness of Method

To be an Aristotelian in 1700 was to assert the primacy and priority of the community over the individual. As Aristotle argued in the *Politics*, the individual, by nature and in his essence, belongs to the polis: we thus

see that the polis exists by nature and that it is prior to the individual. Not being self-sufficient when they are isolated, all individuals are so many parts all equally depending on the whole. The man who is isolated – who is unable to share in the benefits of political association, or who has no need to share because he is already self-sufficient – is no part of the polis and must therefore be either a beast or a god. (1943, I.2, 1252b)

Against the arguments of the sophists and the pre-Socratic materialists, Aristotle asserted that the polis or society is part of nature and thus, like all other things in nature, possesses a proper form. Once the polis is adequate to its essential nature any change is a change for the worse, a corruption.

Similarly the degrees and distinctions internal to human society are themselves inscribed in the natural order. Aristotle attacked the sophists who argued that "the relation of master and slave is due to law or convention; there is no natural difference between them: the relation of master and slave is based on force and being so based has no warrant in justice (*dike*)" (1943, I.2, 123b). In opposition, he argues that

in all cases where there is a compound, constituted of more than one part forming one common entity – whether the parts be continuous (as in the body of a man or discrete (as in the relation of master and slave) – a ruling element and a ruled can always be traced. This characteristic is present in animate beings by virtue of the whole constitution of nature, inanimate as well as animate: for even in things which are inanimate there is a sort of ruling principle, such as is to be found for example, in a musical harmony. (1943, I.5, 1254a)

The notion that the polis or community necessarily pre-exists and is logically prior to the individual is as important in the realm of knowledge as it is in the practical realms of ethics and politics. According to Aristotle, knowledge exists in two forms, neither of which is reducible to, or even founded upon, individual sense-experience (1967, I.1, 100a). Sense experience remains particular, partial and, in and of itself, fragmentary. It is elevated to knowledge only as it becomes generalized in social concourse. Properly human learning takes place by means of discourse between men, and "all teaching and learning through discourse proceed from previous knowledge" (1967, I.1, 100a, 10–30). Further, because the individual can only learn that which is already known and spoken of by cultured men in the polis, Aristotle argues that "before the learner is led on to a thing or acquires syllogistic knowledge, however, perhaps it should be said that in a certain manner he already knows" (1975, I.1, 71a). Thus, knowledge which remains at the level of the individual cannot be distinguished from the "knowledge" (sense-perception and memory) of beasts. Human knowledge only assumes its true nature in discourse, the logos or dialogos that distinguishes man from animal and which is the foundation of the polis (1943, I.2, 1253a, 10–11).

Aristotle begins the *Topics* with the premise that there exist two valid kinds of reasoning. The first employs demonstrations whose premises are "true and primary" (that is, self-evident) and whose conclusions are therefore judged to be certain. This species of reasoning is proper to mathematics and the sciences; it produces an *episteme*. The other valid form of reasoning is the dialectical, which takes as its premises "opinions that are generally accepted" (*ta endoxa*) (1967, I.1, 100a). The phrase "generally accepted" refers, depending on the case, to opinions accepted by "every one" or to those accepted by "the philosophers". In the *Posterior Analytics* Aristotle argues that while demonstrative reasoning is used in the individual sciences, the principles common to science in general – for example, "that everything must either be affirmed or denied or that if equals are taken from equals, the remainders are equal" – are not and cannot be demonstrated by any of the sciences (or the techniques of proof proper to them) (1975, I.3, 72b). Such common principles can only be arrived at by dialectical reasoning which eschews the quest for certainty and which regards its merely "probable" or "commonly accepted" conclusions as certain (Aristotle 1975, I.3, 72b; Aubenque 1962). Aristotle further contends in the *Metaphysics* that to demand a certain demonstration of common principles, such as the principle of non-contradiction, would be to make any demonstration impossible:

> Some indeed from a lack of education demand that this principle too be demonstrated; for it is a lack of education not to know that it is necessary to seek demonstration of some propositions and not of others. For there cannot be a demonstration of everything altogether; there would then be infinite regress and hence still no final demonstration. (1942, III.4, 1006a)

We should note here that Aristotle carried out what Pierre Aubenque has called a "rehabilitation of opinion" in dissenting from Plato (1962, 264). Plato regarded opinion (*doxa*) as one of the chains that held men imprisoned in the underground world of the sensible. It was precisely the dialectic that would lead a few individuals into the light of the intelligible Forms. Just as Aristotle distrusted the distinction between the two worlds (the sensible and the intelligible), so he distrusts the opposition of *doxa* and *episteme* (opinion and knowledge). "It is the mark of a cultured man to look for precision in each class of things just so far as the nature of the subject allows; it is just as foolish to accept probable reasoning from a mathematician as to demand demonstrative proofs from a rhetorician" (1925, I.3, 1094b). The cultured man as such, the man possessed of *paidea*, does not have a single domain that is proper to him, a determinate region of being to which he has been assigned. Rather, his domain is the totality of being in which it is his place to "assign to partial, that is, scientific discourses their place and meaning in the totality" (Aubenque 1962, 260). It is therefore the role of the cultured man to decide when common belief is or is not the appropriate guarantee of knowledge, and correspondingly whether or not a demonstrative proof is possible. Further, men of culture defend the ultimate authority of undemonstrable common beliefs as the necessary condition of any scientific or logical operation whatsoever.

Aristotle or madness: the division of truth into demonstrable and dialectical is rooted in the social order and reflects its hierarchical arrangement, an arrangement that is itself organic and natural. To ignore this order, to demand absolute certainty in every realm of knowledge alike, including those realms that general opinion has placed outside the jurisdiction of demonstration, is to endanger knowledge itself. The price of ignoring the necessary division of knowledge is infinite regression, contradiction, meaninglessness and finally the triumph of nonsense. To place oneself willingly outside the foundations of common belief is to become a beast by trying to be a god, to become illogical by pushing logic beyond its proper domain.

Thus Aristotle's rather mild distinction between the cultured and the uncultured has become, in *A Tale*, the distinction between reason and madness. Swift tells us that the members of the "academy of Modern Bedlam" have sought to know "things agreed on all hands impossible to be known" (1958, 166). They and their followers see themselves as "having generally proceeded in the common course of their words and actions by a method very different from the vulgar dictates of unrefined reason" (166). To abandon the necessary foundations of thought itself as "prejudices" in search of absolute certainty could only lead to infinite regression and endless doubt. The inventors of "new schemes" in philosophy had, by the very fact that they deliberately placed themselves outside the realm of common understanding in order to verify its propositions, placed themselves outside of reason itself in a twilight world of "dreams and visions":

> For the brain in its natural position and state of serenity, disposeth its owner to pass his life in the common forms, without any thoughts of subduing the multitudes to his own power, his reasons or his visions; and the more he shapes his understanding by the pattern of human learning, the less he is inclined to form parties after his particular notion, because that instructs him in his private infirmities, as well as in the stubborn ignorance of the people. But when a man's fancy gets astride on his reason, when imagination is at cuffs with the senses, and common understanding as well as common sense, is kicked out of doors; the first proselyte he makes is himself and when that is once compassed, the difficulty is not so great in bringing over others; a strong delusion always operating from without as vigorously as from within. (1958, 171)

Thus the question of method, far from being restricted to the realm of scientific discovery, had become a singular site of conflict. From Swift's position, the search for a method entailed a series of transgressions against the true order of things beginning in the human mind and ending at the level of society as a whole. The mind abandons its rightful place and the serenity proper to it only if the original hierarchy of its faculties has been overthrown, if fancy has overcome reason and imagination has seceded from common understanding and sense experience; if, finally, the body comes to rule over the soul. The search for a method begins with a rejection of human learning as groundless at the very moment that the search, by positing the individual as the necessary starting point of knowledge, rejects the only true ground for which it can ever hope: the common forms as defined by the everlasting monuments of both Christian and pagan culture. The ordered generality of learning and wisdom gives way to a chaos of particular, individual knowledges, an epistemological war of all against all.

However, the serenity and perfection that the human mind was made for have never existed unchallenged. Philosophy made its appearance in the Greek world not so much in the form of a doctrine as in the form of an ideological counterattack, a defense of a besieged orthodoxy: Plato against the sophists, Aristotle against the materialists. The Bedlam of philosophy is therefore a kind of counter-archive in which are assembled the thinkers who dismissed human learning as "opinion", who asserted the primacy of body over spirit, of the individual over the community.

In the seventeenth century the major frontal assault on the position that man (and by implication, his knowledge) is social in nature was launched by Hobbes (Mintz 1969; Spragens 1973). Against the Anglican orthodoxy of his time, Hobbes argued that society was not part of nature but, rather, composite and artificial in character. Accordingly, society, in order to be understood, must be "resolved into its component parts or atoms" (1968, 100–110). Thus the individual, his nature and his capacities, must logically precede society as the object of knowledge, society being ultimately a combination of individuals. Further, human beings must first be considered only as corporeal beings, subject, like all bodies, to certain laws of motion (Spragens 1973). However, it was Descartes who emerged as the most systematic opponent of the Aristotelianism of his time, contesting the view that mathematical and logical truths coexisted with and even rested upon more fundamental precepts whose sole guarantee was general opinion. Descartes, like the "uncultured men" Aristotle chastises in the *Nicomachean Ethics*, failed to see that specific areas of inquiry possess forms of reason proper to them, and hence he refused the necessary and natural pluralism of reason. In the *Rules for the Direction of the Mind*, Descartes argued that "merely probable knowledge" must be rejected *tout court* and that we must

> make it a rule to trust only what is completely known and incapable of being doubted. No doubt men of education may persuade themselves that there is but little of such knowledge, because forsooth a common failing of human nature has made them deem it too easy and open to everyone and so led them to neglect to think upon such truths; but I nevertheless announce that there are more of these than they think – truths which suffice to give a rigorous demonstration of innumerable propositions, the discussion of which they have hitherto been unable to free from the element of probability. (1985, Vol. 1, 10–11)

Descartes' dream of a *mathesis universalis* did not simply privilege one form of knowledge over others; it placed truths that could not be expressed in mathematical terms outside the realm of knowledge altogether, in a shadowy world of hearsay. Thus, the distinctions of quality internal to being itself, which in turn necessitate different kinds of knowledge and reason, collapse into the uniformity of mere quantities, knowledge of which is achieved through algebraic calculation. From Swift's position, however, the dream of a *mathesis universalis* was a dream within an even more fantastical dream. For, unlike Aristotle, who recognized that the possibility of philosophical discourse and of reason itself depended upon conditions whose validity was founded upon the general agreement that they were necessary starting points to be accepted without apodictic demonstration, Descartes, by rejecting any recourse to general belief, demanded precisely the impossible proof and sought in his own way to furnish it. Underlying the difference in method is the more basic difference over the locus of truth. Swift believed that the community of learning with its archive of eternally valid works was prior to the individual. The community in its generality and commonality was a bulwark against the peculiar weaknesses of an individual thinker. Without this guardrail of reason, enforced by the institutions of Church and State, there was a constant danger of raising the part above the whole, the individual above the community and, at the extreme (which never seems very distant), a danger of regression into senselessness and meaninglessness.

In direct counterpoint Descartes begins the *Discourse on Method* with an architectural metaphor designed to prove the superiority of the individual over the collectivity:

> one of the first considerations that occurred to me was that there is often less perfection in works composed of several portions and carried out by the hands of various masters, than in those on which one individual alone has worked. Thus we see that buildings planned and carried out by one architect alone are usually more beautiful and better proportioned than those which many have tried to put in order and improve, make use of old walls which were built with other ends in view. (1985, Vol. 1, 116)

The history of philosophy resembles a city lacking any unity whatsoever, a chaos of individual dwellings which, despite the excellence of any given construction, does not as a whole constitute a harmonious totality. Philosophy, the production of the many rather than of a single mind, resembles a city in which "large buildings and small buildings [are] indiscriminately placed together, thus rendering the streets crooked and irregular, so that it might be said that it was chance rather than the will of men guided by reason that led to such an arrangement" (116).

For Descartes, "to shape the understanding according to the pattern of human learning", as Swift argued, would not be to imitate the immanent order of a unified *doxa* but rather to surrender to a chaos of irreconcilable opinions. Something like "general opinion" could only be arrived at by tabulating theoretical majorities. Such reasoning can only adduce what has been said by the most authors, producing a plurality of truths, some held by a majority, others by a minority.

> It would be no use to total up the testimonies in favor of each, meaning to follow that opinion which was supported by the greatest number of authors; for if it is a question of difficulty that is in dispute, it is more likely that the truth would have been discovered by a few than by many. But even though all these men agreed among themselves, what they teach would not suffice for us. For we shall not e.g. all turn out to be mathematicians though we know by heart all the proofs that others have elaborated, unless we have an intellectual talent that fits us to resolve difficulties of any kind. Neither though we have mastered all the arguments of Plato and Aristotle if yet we have not the capacity for passing a solid judgement on these matters, shall we become philosophers; we should have acquired the knowledge not of a science, but of history. (116)

There is only one antidote to the chaos of opinions in philosophy: it must be reduced to the simple, singular order of analytic reason. With the exchange of unity for diversity also comes certainty for probability. To be sure, such an improvement in the condition of thought requires a radical cure. To return to Descartes' architectural metaphor, "where there is danger of the houses falling of themselves, and when foundations are not secure", the house itself must be knocked down and rebuilt from scratch. In philosophy an equally destructive method must be employed: universal doubt.

> As regards all the opinions which up to this time I had embraced, I thought I could do no better than endeavor once and for all to sweep them completely away, so that they might later on be replaced, either by others which were better, or by the same when I had made them conform to the uniformity of a rational scheme. (1985, Vol. 1, 117)

For Swift, the madness here is not simply that "Cartesius reckoned to see before he died the sentiments of all philosophers like so many stars in his romantic system, wrapped and drawn within his own vortex" (1958, 167). It is even more that by doubting everything, by tearing down not only the house but its very foundations, Descartes leaves himself no place from which to begin rebuilding the edifice of knowledge. Of course, it could be objected that the method of universal doubt was intended precisely to clear away the decayed, unreliable foundations so as to discover the one point solid enough to support the search for truth: the cogito. From the theoretical position occupied by Swift, however, only the inverse could be true: only the pattern of human learning together with the understanding common to all men could support a search for truth, because this alone can correct the infirmities of any given individual. The cogito therefore was no foundation at all but the opening of an abyss.

We may now see the impossibility of Swift's position. Few of Descartes' critics denied the need for a new method. Fewer still were willing to invoke Aristotle against Cartesian philosophy. Arguments were advanced as to the precise kind of method that was necessary and even as to the extent of the break with prior learning. No one, however, spoke from the point of view of this prior learning. The great objectors to the *Meditations* (Arnauld, Hobbes, Gassendi) were, on the question of breaking with Aristotle, Descartes' allies. Of all the major philosophers of the seventeenth century only one invoked Aristotle's argument against disregarding probable ideas in the search for truth, and this philosopher might well be seen as Swift's other, an inverted image of all that he believed: Spinoza. In the *Treatise on the Emendation of the Intellect*, Spinoza warned against the danger of infinite regress in the search for certainty:

> To find the best method of seeking the truth, there is no need of another method to seek the method of seeking the truth, or of a third method to seek the second, and so on, to infinity. For in that way we would never arrive at knowledge of the truth, or indeed at any knowledge. (1985, 16)

It is to just such an argument that Swift's comments on Descartes in the *Tale* seem to refer. The quest for absolute certainty, for a certainty that disengages itself from general belief finally to oppose it on the mere foundation of the individual cogito, is ultimately nothing more than the dream of certainty of a man who has willfully cast himself into infinite doubt. Because it rejects

59

its rightful social foundation, the search for absolute certainty can have no end: every proof must furnish its own proof *ad infinitum*. Aristotle had long ago refuted Descartes' argument in his critique of the sophists in the *Metaphysics* (Cudworth 1845). Accordingly, at the end of the *Battle of the Books,* an arrow from Aristotle's bow hits Descartes and the pain draws "him into his own vortex" (Swift 1958, 244). No ally, however, could be more unwelcome to Swift than Spinoza. Swift's critique of the search for absolute certainty was not based on a rejection of the need for a secure and enduring foundation for knowledge. The madness of the modern philosophers consisted in their rejection of the only possible guarantee of wisdom: the pattern of human learning and the common understanding upon which it is based. The search for a method is therefore profoundly unnatural, an abandonment of that portion of knowledge proper to the human condition, an elevation of the individual over the community, the part over the whole.

Spinoza's use of Aristotle's argument is characteristically heretical. He invokes the danger of infinite regression not to argue that knowledge as it is constituted is a suitable foundation for further inquiry, but to insist that knowledge neither has nor requires any foundation whatsoever. Truth requires no guarantees: "just as light makes manifest both itself and darkness, so truth is the standard both of itself and of falsity" (1985, 479). To justify his rejection of method, Spinoza takes an example from the history of the mechanical arts:

> to forge iron a hammer is needed, and to have a hammer, it must be made; for this, another hammer and other tools are needed; and to have these tools too, other tools will be needed, and so on to infinity; in this way someone might try, in vain, to prove that men have no power of forging iron.... But just as men, in the beginning, were able to make the easiest things with the tools they were born with (however laboriously and imperfectly) and once these had been made, made other, more difficult things with less labor and more perfectly and so proceeding from the simplest works and tools, reached the point where they accomplished so many and so difficult things with little labor, in the same way the intellect, by its inborn power, makes intellectual tools for itself, by which it acquires other power for other intellectual works, and from these works still other tools. (1985, 16–17)

Knowledge therefore has no true beginning, no point of origin. We have ideas that, no matter how rudimentary, will serve to help us fabricate the truth. The method by which theoretical raw materials are transformed into adequate knowledge can only be known after the fact. Further, as Pierre Macherey comments,

> The ideas with which it is necessary to begin to arrive at knowledge are not innate truths upon which might be founded, once and for all, as if on an immovable base, an order of reasons, but rather a material to be worked, which must be profoundly modified in order subsequently to serve in the production of truths. (1978, 63)

Here, then, was the danger of a direct defense of Aristotle: any attack on the project of a search for a method of discovering the truth risked calling into question the very idea of foundations, guarantees, of all notions of transcendental, enduring truth. To invoke too directly Aristotle's defense of dialectical reasoning was perhaps to open the way to the Spinozist anarchy whose violence had been amply demonstrated in the *Tractatus Theologico-Politicus*. The result could only be a rejection of all authority, whether political, ecclesiastical or even rational in a world without transcendence (Balibar 1989; Moreau 1975; Negri 1991).

II. The Problematization of Spirit

The question of method seemed, in the seventeenth century, inescapably linked to another set of philosophical operations. The frequency and regularity of terms like matter, substance, body and space through the work of Descartes, Hobbes, Gassendi and Spinoza might tempt us to identify in this set, as the orthodox of the time did, a materialism common to these thinkers, a tendency to privilege matter over spirit. We might expand Koyré's description of Cartesian philosophy as a "materialization of space", or Thomas Spragens' description of Hobbes's "corporealisation of substance" to encompass the entire movement (Koyré 1957, 88–109; Spragens 1973, 77–96). Is it the case, however, that the words "matter" or "body" function in an equivalent or analogous way in the work of Descartes and Hobbes? Or that the "substance" referred to in Spinoza's *Ethics* and in Gassendi's *Disquisitio* is identical, equidistant from the substance of scholasticism and the *ousia* of Aristotelianism? It seems more proper to speak rather of a problematization of spirit that unites on a certain plane a number of philosophical utterances in their very dispersion and difference. We must not imagine that these utterances undermined the edifice

61

of spirit to the same degree and with the same efficacy. Even Cudworth, who could assemble Descartes, Hobbes, Gassendi and Hobbes under the rubric "Democritical", took great care to distinguish between these philosophies, the degrees to which they erred, the weight of what was valuable relative to the weight of what was harmful and dangerous. One of the major objectives of Anglican thought at the end of the century was not so much to attack the philosophies of matter as to defend the edifice of spiritual, immaterial substance against an unholy alliance whose strategies were numberless and whose cunning was inexhaustible. Henry More, for example, felt reduced to proving merely

> that the existence of a Spirit or Incorporeal Substance is possible. But there is no reason anyone should wonder that I have spent much pain to make so small and inconsiderable a progress as to bring the thing only to a bare possibility. For though I may have seemed to have gained little to myself, yet I have given a very signal overthrow to the adverse party whose strongest hold seems to be an unshaken confidence that the every notion of a Spirit of Substance immaterial is a perfect incompossibility and pure nonsense. (1925, 86)

Such "bare possibility" must be defended when from the impossibility of incorporeal substance are deduced no better consequences than these:

> That it is impossible that there should be any God or soul or Angel, Good or Bad; or immortality or life to come. That there is no religion, no piety nor impiety, no virtue nor vice, Justice nor injustice, but pleases him that has the longest sword to call so. That there is no freedom of will nor consequently any rational remorse of conscience in any being whatsoever but that all that is, is nothing but matter and corporeal motion; and that therefore every trace of man's life is as necessary as the tracts of lightning and the fallings of thunder, the blind impetus of the matter breaking through or being stopped everywhere, with as certain and determinate necessity as the course of a torrent after mighty storms and showers of rain. (86–7)

For Swift, as for Cudworth and More, Aristotle's system stood as a direct refutation of the materialism of the seventeenth century insofar as Aristotle had already refuted Democritus and Leucippus. Cudworth, for example, while admitting that mechanistic and corpuscular theories seem better able to account for the physical world (Swift admitted as much in *Gulliver's Travels*), argues that "the Aristotelic system is right and sound here as to those greater things; in asserting a Deity distinct from the world, the naturality of morality and liberty of will" (1845, Vol. 1, 95). Hobbes's curt dismissal of Aristotle's *Ethics* and his attempt to replace it with his own

> is nothing but the old Democritic doctrine revived, is no ethics at all but a mere cheat, the undermining and subversion of all morality, by substituting something like it in the room of it, that is a mere counterfeit and changeling; the design whereof could not be any other than to debauch the world. (95)

Indeed, because Aristotle's cosmos (which included both *techne* and *physis*) was ruled by first principles and ultimate ends and possessed a design that was prior to it, the Aristotelian system as a totality remained superior not simply to the Democritical systems associated with the ancient materialists and with Gassendi and Hobbes but even to the

> Cartesian hypothesis itself, which yet plainly supposeth incorporeal substance. For as much as this latter makes God contribute nothing more to the fabric of the world, than the turning round of a vortex or whirlpool of matter; from the fortuitous motion of which according to the general laws of nature must proceed all this frame of things that now is, the exact organization and successive generation of animals, without the guidance of any mind or wisdom. Whereas Aristotle's nature is no fortuitous principle, but such as doth nothing in vain but all for ends and in everything pursues the best; and therefore can be no other than a subordinate instrument of the divine wisdom and the manuary officer or executioner of it. (95)

The embattled orthodoxy of the late seventeenth century saw in the problematization of spirit, a madness. Cudworth argued that

> as the physicians speak of a certain disease or madness, called hydrophobia, the symptom of those who have been bitten by a mad dog which makes them have a monstrous antipathy to water; so all atheists are possessed with a certain kind of madness, that may be called pneumatophobia that makes them have an irrational but desperate abhorrence from spirits or incorporeal substances, they being acted also at the same time with hylomania, whereby they madly dote upon numen. (200)

Like all forms of madness, hylomania disturbs the actions of the senses and the exercise of reason; ultimately it makes knowledge impossible: "and indeed if there were no other being in the world but individual matter and all knowledge proceeded from the impresses of that matter, that being always agitated, it is not conceivable how there could be any stability of knowledge any more than of essence found in the rapid whirlpool of corporeal things; nay nor how there should be any such thing as knowledge at all" (95).

Hylomania is in fact the species of madness that is exhibited throughout the *Tale*. We have seen that Swift's attack on the "mad philosophers" is launched from the Aristotelian position that the universe is teleologically ordered. The mind has its natural position in which it may find a state of serenity. The importance of common understanding itself rests on the fact that the polity within which it exists is itself "natural" and thereby divinely ordained. To reject or even to call into question the idea of incorporeal or spiritual substance is to remove the very possibility of order from the world. Nature would then become matter in motion without beginning, end or purpose. Society, whatever its particular form, would have no state proper to it. It could be nothing more than what has been agreed upon by the many, or forced by the strong.

The reception of Descartes' work in England in the second half of the seventeenth century is particularly revealing. The *Meditations* and *The Principles of Philosophy* were initially greeted with alacrity as a defense of theism and the notion of immaterial substance in opposition to Hobbes and the Epicurean revival associated with Gassendi (Nicholson 1929, 348–66). In the face of arguments that all human knowledge was ultimately derived from and reducible to the senses, which in turn simply received the impression of external matter in motion, Descartes argued that the mind as *res cogitans* is more easily knowable than things of the body as *res extensa*. In fact, Descartes discovered that, in the crucible of doubt, his existence is reduced "in the strict sense" to that of "a thing which thinks". It is the cogito's knowledge of itself which constitutes that which alone may not be doubted. While, in the second meditation, thought discovers within itself a clear and distinct idea of extension (the piece of wax), it finds (in the third meditation) that it cannot be absolutely certain of the external existence of any extended thing unless God is first established as the guarantor of knowledge. Even systematic doubt itself presupposes an idea of

God: "For how could I understand that I doubted or desired – that is, lacked something – and that I was not wholly perfect unless there were in me some idea of a more perfect being which enabled me to recognize my own defects by comparison?" (1985, Vol. 2, 122).

Descartes seemed "an antidote to Atheism", an alternative to the sensualism and materialism of Gassendi. But the antidote soon seemed rather a poison than a cure. The Cartesian division of the world into two distinct realms – extended (material) and un-extended (spiritual) substance – functioned as a compromise, an attempt to render the materialism of philosophical and scientific inquiry compatible with (or at least not antagonistic to) religious doctrine. Extended substance was bound by laws and subject to an absolute determinism, while the *res cogitans* was defined by its freedom from the constraints that bound the material world. But matter had been detached so radically from spirit that the material world functioned autonomously and spirit seemed positively superfluous, not so much trapped in matter as excluded from it, exiled from the world. Thus Pascal regarded infinite Galilean spaces and saw only the absence of God (Althusser 1989, 121). The world no longer exhibited *vestigia Dei*, but only signs of his absence. The sage could no longer discern the unending murmur of the divine logos but only the eternal silence of dead matter. Henry More called Descartes a "nullibist": because God was un-extended he could not be said to exist *in* the universe; in fact, he existed nowhere, *nullibi* (184). Indeed, not only had Descartes re-moved God from the world, he declared that the empty spaces that He might inhabit were not empty at all but filled with vor-tices of subtle matter. Thus, God was not only banished from the world, but the void that he left behind, which might have (as for Pascal) declared his absence, was filled. As Koyré remarks,

> in spite of his having invented or perfected the magnificent a priori proof of the existence of God which Henry More embraced enthusias-tically and was to maintain all his life, Descartes, by his teaching, leads to materialism and by his exclusion of God from the world, to atheism. From now on, Descartes and the Cartesians are to be relentlessly criti-cized and to bear the derisive nickname of nullibists. (1957, 138)

The priority of spirit over matter was logical not ontological, a priority in reason not in existence. What was at first seen as the spiritual foundation of truth was soon revealed to have been nothing but a ladder to certain knowledge about the material world which, once it was scaled, could then be discarded. Incorporeal and unextended substance in general and God in particular remained radically external to the material world, whose workings could be explained only by causes internal to it. The search for final causes had to be abandoned; only material and efficient causes could be known.

For many thinkers, the sinister destiny of the Cartesian apparatus was confirmed by a philosopher who was rash enough to take certain of Descartes' arguments to extreme conclusions: Spinoza. The fragile compromise that united the otherwise incompatible segments of Cartesian philosophy, and which thus made it at least initially acceptable to the established order, was shattered forever by the relentless demonstrations of the *Ethics*. Speaking or seeming to speak the language of Descartes, Spinoza "solved" the problem of dual substances by breaking decisively with the very framework of Cartesian doctrine. In 1641 Gassendi and Hobbes, in their objections to the *Meditations*, rejected Descartes' claim to have demonstrated the existence of a *res cogitans* distinct from the *res extensa*. Both philosophers argued that Descartes' theses could only lead to the conclusion that it is extended matter itself that thinks. Hobbes turned Descartes' own example of the piece of wax against him. If it is true that matter retains its identity through whatever modifications it undergoes and thought is simply one of these modifications, from "the fact that we cannot separate thought from a matter that thinks, the proper inference seems to be that that which thinks is material rather than immaterial" (Descartes, 1985, Vol. 2, 122). However, the critique of dualism occupied a minor place in Hobbes's philosophical project and Gassendi drew back from the positions advanced in the *Disquitio Metaphysica* (his response to Descartes) as if from a precipice (Bloch 1971). It was thus left to Spinoza to prove *in modo scribendi geometrico* not simply the impossibility of there existing more than one substance but the scandalous political, theological and moral implications of this critique.

Rosalie L. Colie has shown that just as the diseases of Hobbesism and Cartesianism were felt to have been eradicated, the publication of Spinoza's *Tractatus Theologico-Politicus* and shortly afterward the *Opera Postuma* appeared to signal the emergence of an even more resilient strain of atheism (Colie 1963). At the very time Swift was writing the *Tale*, a succession of leading Anglican thinkers attacked Spinozism in the Boyle Lectures (1695–1706) as the most systematic and internally consistent critique of the reigning ideas (Colie 1963).

One of the particular forms that the general problematization of incorporeal substance took was a newly felt difficulty in explaining the precise relation of God to the created world. Two lines of argumentation developed: (1) God is the cause of the world to be sure, but an external cause whose relation to its effects the age described as "transitive" or "mechanical"; (2) in order for God not to be simply Aristotle's *primum mobile*, He must be seen as an expressive or emanative cause whose essence is manifest in all created phenomena. The first argument, associated with Descartes, Hobbes and Gassendi, was criticized for rendering God irrelevant and superfluous, a creator who had constructed a machine so perfect in its workings that his presence was no longer necessary or, more importantly, no longer evident. The second argument, associated with Hermetic currents, and to some extent with the Cambridge Platonists, saw God's essence expressed in the created world, which in turn participated in God. However, as Gilles Deleuze has shown, the conception of expression introduced a separation between God and creation, between spirit and matter, that constantly threatened to become absolute. The distance between appearance and essence, between surface and depth might become so great that any connection between the two terms would become impossible, producing the unthinkable: appearance without essence, surface without depth. Spinoza's conception of God as the cause immanent in its effects appeared to his horrified contemporaries to be just that.

Spinoza began his argument in the *Ethics* with the anti-dualist proposition that "in the universe, there cannot be two or more substances of the same nature or attribute" (1985, 411). The notion of the world as one substance dispels the problem of the radical exteriority of a spiritual substance to the material world: "one substance cannot be produced by another substance" (411). The ideas fundamental to Christianity of God's separation from the world and His creation *ex nihilo* are rejected. Furthermore, because "existence belongs to the nature of substance" and because substance is infinite, the theory of creation per se is false along with the important notions of possible and potential existences (as in the idea of Divine Providence) (412). There is nothing of God apart from the world; no potential or power apart from actual existence because God is no more than the totality of what is, of actual existence (*Deus sive Natura*), and he has no power to make of the world (which is identical to God himself) other than what it is.

From the arguments against dualism, Spinoza turned to the task of locating and defining God. In doing so, he arrived at what has often been seen as a species of Neo-Platonic pantheism. Since there exists only "substance consisting of infinite attributes", and "there can be or be conceived no other substance but God", then "whatever is, is in God and nothing can be or be conceived without God" (412). Spinoza's argument seems to leave room for a power or even simply a teleology absolutely immanent in being, distinct from which nothing could exist. However, most of his contemporaries saw the *Ethics* as the systematic elimination of every argument for spirit whether transcendent or immanent. Spinoza constructed a material God that could in no way be prior to or separate from that which he has "created" and who further has no power to make of the world other than what it is (420). Thus Spinoza portrayed a world without room for God, without even the infinite empty spaces that marked for Pascal God's absence. Spinoza's world was a plenitude of substance without spirit and thus without beginning or end, without prior purpose or ultimate goal, substance which renewed itself in infinitely diverse forms (Macherey 1978; Negri 1991).

Unlike Descartes, Hobbes and Gassendi, Spinoza did not hesitate to draw the most radical conclusions from the singular materialism presented in Book I of the *Ethics*. In the Appendix to Book I, he argues that since there can exist no potential existences, since all that can exist does, there can be nothing like a goal either of human history or of nature and no ultimate ends or ideal states: "Nature has no fixed goal and . . . all final causes are but figments of human imagination" (1985, 442). The doctrine of final causes presupposes that nature (or God) is impelled towards that which it lacks or towards a state of perfection in relation to which it must be said to be imperfect. But, Spinoza argues, all that exists is perfect in the sense that existence is its sole model and type, for there neither is nor could be conceived any thing outside of, transcendental to, or even immanent in, substance: "the perfection of things should be measured solely from their own nature and power" (544).

68

In the preface to Book IV, Spinoza takes this line of thought several steps further to attack the very ideas of perfection, ideal types, and models:

> Men are wont to form general ideals both of natural phenomena and of artifacts and these ideas they regard as models, and they believe that nature (which they consider does nothing without an end in view) looks to these ideas and holds them before her as models. So when they see something occurring in Nature at variance with their preconceived ideal of the thing in question, they believe that nature has then failed or blundered and has left that thing imperfect. So we see that men are in the habit of calling natural phenomena perfect or imperfect from their own preconception rather than from true knowledge.... The reason or cause why God or nature acts and the reason why he exists are one and the same. Therefore just as he does not exist for an end, so he does not act for an end; just as there is no beginning or end to his existing; so there is no beginning or end to his acting. (544)

By attacking all notions of transcendental norms or fixed ends, Spinoza undercuts the very possibility of satire, insofar as satire exhibits the inadequacy of what exists in relation to what could or should exist. The actions and practices of men have not been understood for what they are in themselves, but have been attacked and criticized for failing to correspond to what does not in fact exist, a non-existent model.

> Philosophers conceived of the passions which harass us as vices into which men fall by their own fault and therefore generally deride, bewail or blame them or execrate them if they wish to seem unusually pious. And so they think they are doing something wonderful and reaching the pinnacle of learning when they are clever enough to bestow manifold praise on such human nature as is nowhere to be found and to make verbal attacks on that which in fact exists. For they conceive of men not as they are but as they themselves would like them to be. Whence it has come to pass that instead of ethics they have generally written satire and that they have never conceived a theory of politics which could be turned to use, but such as might be taken for a chimera or might have been formed in a utopia or in that golden age of the poets where, to be sure, there was least need of it. (1951, 287)

But the attack on dualism (for dualism, whether Cartesian or not, preserved spirit in some form) went even further in the *Ethics*, questioning the very possibility of a relation between mind and body or at least a causal, not to say, intentional relation between them. To begin with, the *Ethics* rejects the idea of free will and in particular the idea of the individual subject of knowledge and action. Human thought and conduct have too long been seen as "phenomena outside nature" which therefore exist independently of natural determinations and laws. The traditional notion of man as "a kingdom within a kingdom" with "absolute power over his actions" has prevented an adequate understanding of the laws and necessities that govern not only man's activities but also his emotions and passions (1985, 491).

One of the most durable illusions underlying the general misconception of human nature is the domination of mind over body. Whereas Descartes retreated from the vision of an undisturbed parallelism between the two substances, Spinoza characteristically took things to the extreme to insist that "the body cannot determine the mind to think nor can the mind determine the body to motion or rest " (494). With Spinoza, therefore, spirit disappeared into substance, and transcendence was eliminated. What foundation could there be for the institutions and practices of men in a world without transcendence? The truth of this world precisely lay outside of and beyond it; matter possessed meaning only insofar as it was shaped, formed and guided according to a will that was necessarily immaterial and therefore separate from the world. The body itself possessed worth only to the extent that it was inhabited and governed by an incorporeal soul (together with the faculties of understanding and will).

Swift's *Tale* turns repeatedly, inescapably, upon the nightmare of a merely material world, a world from which every trace of spirit has been eliminated (or which in another sense has been utterly eliminated by spirit, as its dregs, its feces). Images of surfaces without depth, bodies without souls, traverse the *Tale* from end to end. Swift's hylophobia develops in two opposing directions. On the one hand, it is the absence of spirit that is explored, a hollowness and emptiness, an internal abyss that mirrors the infinite spaces that surround man. On the other hand, it is the Spinozist plenitude in which all that can exist does, a world which is sufficient to itself even as it undergoes transformation, never evolving towards a *telos*, but in an infinity of forms each of which is its own norm, a full world without spirit, without beginning or end or purpose.

III. The Material Voice

It is no longer simply that the divine logos cannot be heard; it is rather that the world, once the book in which the word might be read, has become silent, opaque and utterly solid. Even language, which in its relation to the human mind served as an analogical explanation of the world's origin in God's mind, has closed upon itself, settling upon its materiality. Human speech and writing no longer seem to express the world of things, but have rather become a part of it, things among others. They resist the imprint of the human mind, and elude its authority. The seventeenth century turned its gaze upon the words themselves, upon their internal order, their history. The truth of a discourse was no longer its correspondence to the world beyond it, but rather the relation between its terms. Truth was enclosed within discourse itself, no longer expressing the adequation of proposition and world. To the consternation of the orthodox, both in England and on the Continent, a few of the most heretical philosophers turned their attention to the Holy Scripture itself. Rejecting the idea of the Bible's perfection and coherence, Hobbes and Spinoza sought, in its contradictions and inconsistencies, the signs of its historicity, that is, the causes of its existence as an artifact fashioned by human hands.

If the ensemble of discourses on matter and spirit in the seventeenth century tended towards the constitution of a world without spirit and thus without ultimate ends or a separate, free intellect, the very notion of truth could not itself escape transformation. In fact, the concepts, notions and terms that governed the discussion of the relationship of language to being, the function of propositional statements, and finally the nature of language itself, were subject to a reordering and redistribution. The conceptual hierarchies of the past continued to survive in the face of this theoretical rearrangement, but their jurisdiction was more narrowly restricted. Truth, for example, continued to be the name of the object that thought was exercised to obtain, but the eternal truth of essences (and not simply the quiddity of the scholastics but also the "immutable essences and true natures" upon which Cudworth insisted), the truth of ultimate purposes and ends, now coexisted with another truth, the truth of appearances and surfaces. In the "Digression concerning Madness" Swift notes that his contemporaries prefer "that wisdom that converses about the surfaces to that pretended philosophy which enters into the depth of things and then comes gravely back with information and discoveries that in the inside they are good for nothing" (1958, 173). It is not so much the attenuation or abandonment of truth as the designation of a truth of superficies that was previously unthinkable. Geometry was a knowledge of surfaces, and the philosophy that modelled itself upon it tended to privilege surfaces over depth, appearance over essence, so that Hobbes might dismiss the question of essence as "a mere nonsense". Swift has registered the possible effects of the nominalist strain in seventeenth-century thought by characteristically pushing it to extreme conclusions, setting it as always against the Aristotelian notion that wisdom seeks to penetrate appearances to grasp the true essence (*ousia*) of things.

Of all the major philosophers of the time, it was Gassendi in an early work, *Exercises Against the Aristotelians*, who sought to open the way to this second truth, the truth of appearances, by opening a breach in the armature of Aristotelian philosophy. Deploying arguments taken from the other antiquity (not so much Democritus as the ancient skeptics, Pyrrho and Sextus Empiricus), Gassendi argues that while Aristotelian philosophy has always sought to "explain what is hidden" and "to make clear what is obscure, the various methods employed to this end can only fail. The techniques of logic and dialectic, definition of the object in question, a division of the whole into its parts, and finally the distinguishing of truth from falsehood, can only restate what appearances tell us. We can only prove what we already know – that, for example, the sun is hot or that it emits light – but no amount of reasoning will take us to its innermost substance" (Gassendi 1972, 84).

Further, the essence of things, their quiddity, the universal ground that makes the existence of particular individuals possible, does not exist in being at all but only in language. At this point Gassendi defends what he fears is considered the "mad opinion of the nominalists", that there exists "no universality outside of thoughts and names" (90). Nominalism thus converged with materialism to produce a world of existence without essence, filled in turn with an infinite series of singularities no longer anchored to stable universal essences, natures, or ultimate ends. To the orthodox, this was truly a nightmarish vision. As Pascal put it in the *Pensées*, "true nature being lost, everything becomes its own true nature; and the true good being lost everything becomes its own true good" (1966, 426). Because no form of knowledge will deliver eternal verities to us, and further, because universal essences are not to be formed in nature but only added to it by language, Gassendi concludes that "knowledge derived from our experience of the appearances of things should be termed genuine knowledge" (1972, 86).

Finally, Gassendi ingeniously sets the chain of being against the very conceptual regime that makes it possible to privilege appearance over essence and surface over depth.

> Nature has indeed instilled the desire to know in all men, but not however the desire to know all things in every way. Now as long as all men desire to know as much as possible either according to experience or within the limitations of appearances, it is true that they desire to know these things at nature's prompting; but as soon as they claim to know other things beyond those, either inner natures or necessary causes, that is the sort of knowledge that belongs to angelic natures or even to the divinity and is not proper for paltry men. Consequently, the desire cannot come from nature. (103–4)

Thus the notion of the essence of the nature of man is deployed against itself: it is man's nature not to know his true nature, the very existence of which therefore becomes superfluous because it cannot figure in our thought or action. It is no wonder that Cudworth feared the ruses of atheism.

Gassendi's rehabilitation of certain nominalist positions opened a space for the more extreme arguments that Hobbes advanced in the sections on speech in *De Corpore* and *Leviathan*. The nominalist notion that the "word universal is never the name of anything existent in nature nor of any idea or phantasm formed in the mind, but always the name of some word or name" (1962, 37) instead of merely serving to distinguish the representative function of universal and particular names or signs permitted a rethinking of the nature of language itself that even as "modern" a thinker as Antoine Arnauld denounced as "very dangerous" (1970, 10). The danger that Arnauld perceived was the reordering of the hierarchical relations that had bound the terms *language, being* and *truth* together since the time of Aristotle. The concept of language and the possibility of truthful communication seemed inescapably to depend on the notion that just as *veritatus est adequatio rei ad intellectum* (Thomas Aquinas) so a proposition was true if it corresponded to the world of "things" (*rei*). Thus, for Hobbes to argue that "names are not signs of things" and that "a proposition is a speech consisting of two names copulated" seemed to render the relation between speech and the world that it supposedly represented tenuous and problematic. In fact, Hobbes is equivocal on this point both in *De Corpore* and *Leviathan*. One commentator has suggested that his nominalism is at certain points constrained or interrupted by the mechanist strain in his thought (Gargani 1971, 173–97).

But Hobbes's statement on truth, however inconsistent and incomplete the chain of arguments of which it was the conclusion, appeared to Arnauld to border on madness: "True and false are attributes of speech, not of things. And where speech is not, there is neither truth nor falsehood" (1968, 105). Truth, Hobbes went on to say, "consisteth in the right ordering in our affirmation" (105). A world of matter in motion, without incorporeal essences and thus without final causes, no longer expressed a presence prior to itself. Law and right were not found in nature but rather added to it. The truth and adequacy of human institutions could no longer be judged on the basis of their correspondence to nature. An entire chain of correspondences was thus disrupted and the final link of the chain was speech itself. Language no longer named the world, it no longer depended on an existence prior to itself before which it had simply to efface itself for meaning and truth to become manifest. Speech was, to use a phrase associated with Spinoza, "parallel" to the world but not reducible to it. "Peter for example is something real; but a true idea of Peter is an objective essence of Peter and something real in itself and altogether different from Peter himself" (Spinoza 1985, Vol. 1, 17). The very idea of the naming or representational function of language was thus called into question and subjected to a process of rethinking. Speech undoubtedly named a world, the world of things, that was itself real. But naming no longer described a correspondence or a representation of things by words. Instead, the truth and adequacy of language was internal to it, dependent not on the existence of a world outside language but on the objective existence of language itself. The view of language as a spiritual, intellectual essence gave way to a notion of its materiality and solidity. Speech was no longer reducible to something more real but was rather itself fully real and irreducible. It was only in the disposition of the elements of speech that truth was to be found. It is important, finally, to note that there is not the slightest trace of idealism in the philosophical tendency we have described. Far from the world disappearing into thought or language, far from the world losing its materiality to the ideality of thought and speech, thought and language themselves, the last refuges of spirit, congealed into matter, their transparency resolved into the opaque solidity of yet further surfaces without depth, existences without essence.

The orthodox of the time (including Swift himself) often satirized the notion of the materiality of speech by reducing materiality to mere corporeality. The voice becomes a movement of subtle matter, and writing is nothing more than ink on paper. But we have seen that the materiality of speech did not take the form of a reduction or constriction but rather was an expansion that granted speech the objective existence that had been refused it before. Here, as in other domains, the distention of the horizon of intelligibility threatened to upset the very foundations of the dominant conceptual regime. Further, it was as if those who contributed to the emergence of this new concept of speech, especially Hobbes and Spinoza, sought to provide the proof of the revolutionary (or destructive) possibilities inherent in the consideration of speech in its materiality by turning their theoretical apparatus on what once had been an unassailable fortress of the mystery of spirit: The Holy Scripture.

Phillip Harth has described at some length one of the major confrontations regarding Scripture in the seventeenth century (1961, 38–40). He has shown the difficult middle course that Anglican thought (epitomized by Hooker) attempted to negotiate between the interpretive excesses of Rome and the austere literality of Geneva. The relevance of this controversy for the *Tale* (especially the allegory of the three brothers) is beyond doubt. And yet a historically overlapping but quite distinct controversy involving the interpretation of Scripture may prove to have been equally necessary to the appearance of the *Tale*.

In the letter to Francis Godolphin that served as a preface to *Leviathan*, Hobbes expressed his fear that of all that the work contains "that which perhaps may most offend, are certain texts of Holy Scripture alledged by me to other purpose than ordinarily they use to be by others" (1968, 76). Apart from the questions of a few heretical interrogators of the Scriptures, the Bible was held to be the direct transcription of the Holy Word and as such, as Hooker put it, was with "absolute perfection framed" (1969, 214). If contradiction or inconsistencies appeared in the letter of the text, a hermeneutic or interpretive strategy was deployed to restore the text to its original purity. Apparent contradictions were merely metaphors (the purposes of which in Scripture had been explained in detail by Thomas Aquinas) (1964, I.Q. 1, Art. 10). In fact, Spinoza argued in his *Tractatus Theologico-Politicus*, the entire history of both Jewish and Christian scriptural interpretations could be understood as a succession of attempts to deny or explain away what the Bible truly was: a composite, complex and utterly disordered work, which far from representing the Divine Word in its purity and its eternal truth, was an all too human text, fashioned by many hands in many different epochs.

Unlike Spinoza, Hobbes neither differentiated himself systematically from the various interpretive traditions nor did he construct a new method of reading the Scripture (although a method could probably be disengaged from his discussion of the Bible and reconstructed as a theory). In fact, some of his arguments are themselves quite traditional in method, if not exactly in content. When he advances his interpretation of the word "spirit", for example, as necessarily referring to something corporeal, he has simply enlisted in the ranks of those who, as Spinoza put it, twisted Scripture to conform to a philosophical system external to it. What is new in Hobbes's treatment of the Bible is something quite different: it is his scrutiny of the text itself without regard to what lies behind or within it, his granting to the text an irreducibility and a materiality. Earlier commentators regarded the Scripture as a conduit to something greater; like Jacob's ladder, it allowed man to ascend from earth to Heaven. For Hobbes, however, the Bible led nowhere, named nothing, veiled no truths; it was an object itself among other objects to be studied, measured, weighed, mapped. Accordingly, in the famous Chapter 33 of *Leviathan* he applies to the Bible the very same resoluto-compositive method through which nature is known. He divides Scripture into its elements, and inquires into the "number, Antiquity, Scope, Authority and Interpreters of the books of Holy Scripture" (1968, 415). Because the Holy Scripture is not the direct expression of God but, rather, God's word as it was spoken to the prophets and the Apostles, it remains to be determined what God has said to whom and when. Further, before these problems can themselves be addressed, we must acquire some knowledge of how these events were transcribed.

As the words of the Bible, and the propositions into which they are arranged, cease any longer to reveal or conceal mysteries deeper than themselves, but instead congeal into objects which can be investigated, the contradictory and inconsistent character of Scripture is placed in stark relief. The Pentateuch, for example, was said to have been written by Moses, but, as Hobbes argues:

> we read in the last chapter of Deuteronomy, ver. 6 concerning the Sepulcher of Moses, that no man knoweth of his sepulcher, to this day, that is, to the day wherein those words were written. It is therefore manifest that those words were written after his interment. For it were a strange interpretation, to say Moses spoke of his own sepulcher (though by Prophecy) that it was not found to that day, wherein he was not being. (417)

Once Moses' authorship of the Pentateuch is rejected, a series of consequences follows. Similar inconsistencies and problems can be found in the books attributed to the prophets. With its authorship in question, it is clear that Scripture did not survive the ages in a pure state. The more closely it is examined, the more closely we judge the internal disposition of its elements, the more the composite nature of Scripture becomes apparent. It is torn with conflicting doctrines and ideas; it presents conflicting views of the history of the Jews. Any attempt to restore Scripture to its purity (for example, Erasmus or Luther) is doomed to failure. Its faults cannot be attributed merely to its translators; on the contrary, they are proper to the Scripture the very authenticity of which itself can never definitively be established.

Hobbes's treatment of Scripture takes on its full significance only when it converges with the general political line of *Leviathan*. Because the Scripture is traversed with innumerable mysteries which are, by their historical nature, undecidable and un-interpretable (they are indices of its compositiveness and the ir-reducible complexity of its parts), the authority over meaning must be conferred upon the established Church of a Christian common-wealth: "For, whosoever hath a lawful power over any writing, to make it law, hath the power also to approve or disapprove the interpretation of the same" (427). Hobbes thus employed a rudimentary, undeveloped method of reading Scripture to uncover irreconcilable, contradictory and insoluble mysteries; he is willing to consider the historicity of Scripture insofar as it can be made to serve this end. However, he must suspend his search for method at precisely this point because to proceed any further towards a rationality proper to the interpretation of Scripture (which would, by the very nature of reason, be in the capacity of any man) would undercut and subvert the very authority whose existence the mystery of Scripture justifies and makes necessary.

Spinoza, the enemy of mysteries and opponent of servitude, was free from the constraints that prevented Hobbes from developing an interpretive method. In Chapters 7 to 15 of the *Tractatus Theologico-Politicus*, Spinoza systematically differentiates both his concept of Scripture and his method of interpreting it from those of his predecessors. We saw that Hobbes's nominalism allowed him to grant Scripture a certain materiality, at least to the extent that it could be broken down into elements and the ordering of these elements noted. Spinoza, however, pushes nominalism to an extreme, granting Scripture a materiality that is equivalent to that of nature itself. Accordingly, he argues that

> the method of interpreting Scripture does not differ widely from method of interpreting nature – in fact it is almost the same. For as the interpretation of nature consists in the examination of the history of nature and therefrom deducing definitions of natural phenomena on certain fixed axioms, so scriptural interpretation proceeds by the examination of Scripture and inferring the intention of its authors as a legitimate conclusion from its fundamental principles. By working in this manner everyone will always advance without danger of error – that is, if they admit no principle for interpreting Scripture and discussing its contents save such as they find in Scripture itself. (1951, 99)

Just as the truth of nature is to be sought in nature itself, in its very materiality and not beyond it, behind it or hidden within it, a spiritual core enclosed in a covering of matter, so is the truth of Scripture to be deduced from the letter of the text itself, not from the Holy Word that is supposedly concealed within it. The being of the text itself, without reference to truths prior to it, must be established. A recent commentary on Spinoza argues that "It is not nature that is a book written by the Divine Logos hailing its creation. It is scripture that is a natural reality that must be described on the basis of its constitutive data and defined genetically on the basis of its formative elements" (Tosel 1984, 61; Zac 1965).

How may we define the irreducible materiality of Scripture, and what are the elements that constitute it? Spinoza cites three elements, the consideration of which is necessary to an adequate knowledge of Scripture. First is "the nature and properties of the language in which the books of the Bible were written and in which their authors were accustomed to speak" (1951, 101). Therefore "a knowledge of Hebrew is before all things necessary" (101). It is important here to distinguish Spinoza's project from those of Erasmus and Luther, both of whom sought to correct the impurities of the Vulgate Bible and to restore the Scripture to its original uncorrupted state. For Spinoza's method leads in precisely the opposite direction. Of the Hebrew language itself only fragments remain. "The meaning of many nouns and verbs which occur in the Bible are either lost or are subjects of dispute. And not only are these gone, but we are lacking in a knowledge of Hebrew idioms" (108). Further, a knowledge of Hebrew reveals that the language in which the Bible was composed had no vowels. The points and accents that substitute for vowels "were invented and designed by men of an after age" (109). In addition, sentences and clauses within sentences were not originally separated by any marks. These, too, were added to the Scripture by later generations. Therefore a knowledge of Hebrew, far from allowing us to recapture the purity of text, instead forces us to confront the fact that the order and consistency of its mode of expression have been added to the text, are thus foreign to it and are not properties that can be discovered in the Scripture.

The second procedure proper to a knowledge of Scripture is to construct its subject matter and the ambiguous and contradictory treatments various subjects receive in the Scripture. Here, as in the investigation of nature, the task is to describe and explain what exists. Because the textual surface of Scripture is traversed with thematic contradictions, and contradictions have traditionally been seen as faults inconsistent with the divine origin and inspiration of the Scripture, previous interpretations with few exceptions have turned away from the task of description to avoid attributing to the Scripture the disorder that it actually possesses. Instead, they chose to explain away and resolve contradictions, declaring them merely apparent. Such an incorrect approach to Scripture is based on the fact that the interpretations have sought not the meaning of the text but its truth, seeking not to consider it in its irreducibility, but rather to reduce it to presences external to it. In contrast, Spinoza proposes "a reason acknowledging no foundation but Scripture itself" (101).

Such a rationality must not begin with the positing of a fictitious or (what amounts to the same thing for Spinoza) externally constructed meaning to which Scripture is made to conform through an obscuring and distorting of the words and propositions that comprise it. Rather, it begins with a rigorous noting of contradictory themes, ideas and passages. Spinoza takes the example of Moses' statements "God is a fire" and "God is jealous". That these statements not only are incompatible but also contradict Moses' assertions in numerous other passages that God has no likeness to any visible thing posed no problem for prior interpretation, whose very reason for being was to explain away such contradictions as "metaphors". Spinoza reminds us, however, that the notion that the Scripture contains a homogeneous and unified doctrine is not to be found in Scripture itself but is derived from sources external to it. Therefore we cannot assume that contradictory assertions in the Bible can necessarily be resolved or harmonized. First, we must ask if the word "fire" possesses other meanings than

> ordinary natural fire. If no such second meaning can be found, the text must be taken literally, however repugnant to reason it may be: and all other passages though in complete accordance with reason, must be brought into harmony with it. If the verbal expressions would not admit of being thus harmonized we should have to set them down as irreconcilable and suspend our judgements concerning them. (102)

The existence of irreconcilable contradiction in the Scripture itself makes necessary the third and final procedure proper to the knowledge of Scripture, one which seeks

> the life, the conduct and the studies of the author of each book, who he was and what was the occasion and the epoch of his writing, whom did he write for and in what language. Further, it should inquire into the fate of each book: how it was first received, into whose hands it fell, how many different versions there were of it, by whose advice was it received into the Bible and lastly how all the books now universally accepted as sacred were united into a single whole. (103)

Contradictory and incompatible assertions and propositions are signs of the history of the Scripture as a material artifact, the historical and authorial diversity of its origin and the transformations it has undergone as a text. Further, Spinoza finds that "the prophets themselves did not agree" on such fundamental notions as "the nature of God, His manner of regarding and providing for things, and similar doctrines" (104). Doctrinal conflicts must therefore be explained but not explained away for the Bible to be truly understood.

Spinoza takes the example of Christ's statement, "But if a man strike you on the right cheek, turn to him the left also." The statement constitutes an abrogation of the law of Moses, the notion that "an eye should be given for an eye". Forsaking any attempt to distort these counterposed moralities into agreement, Spinoza accepts the conflict as a given, as irreducible, and proceeds to explain it, to seek its causes. He finds that whereas Moses "strove to found a well-ordered commonwealth and to ordain laws as a legislator", Christ's precept of "submission to injuries was only valid in places where justice is neglected and in a time of oppression but does not hold good in a well-ordered state" (105). With this demonstration the full import of Spinoza's interpretive method emerges in a clear and distinct form. A thorough knowledge of Hebrew (despite the difficulty of the task given the state of seventeenth-century Hebrew scholarship even among the Jews themselves) allows a careful charting of the surface of the text whose features yield themselves only to such informed scrutiny. Those who based their "deep" interpretations of the Bible on the text of a translation whose accuracy they could not judge were simply constructing hermeneutic edifices on the phantasmatic foundation of their own ignorance. It was precisely because they could not see the text clearly (the meaning of its words, the grammatical structure of its utterances) that they felt the need to "interpret" it (that is, add to it what they could not find) in the first place. Of course there have been interpreters whose errors could not be attributed either to their ignorance of the Hebrew language or to their failure closely to examine the text as it is given. Spinoza takes up the doctrines of two such men and examines them in some depth: Moses Maimonides and Jehuda Alpakhar (an opponent of Maimonides). Both noted the presence of conflicts and inconsistencies in the text of the Scripture but evolved methods of interpretation that sought to restore Scripture to a state of undisturbed harmony, and thus regarded contradictions as blemishes to be removed from the visage of the text through the edifying procedure of interpretation. Maimonides, for example, supposes that the prophets were in entire agreement with one another and that they were consummate philosophers and theologians; for he would have them base their conclusion on the absolute truth. Further, he supposed that the sense of Scripture cannot be made plain from Scripture itself ... and must not be sought there. (117)

Because Maimonides begins with the presupposition (not derived from the text itself) that the Scripture contains no contradictions, he must reconcile the conflicts that are to be found there by appeal to a "higher court", that is, reason. The Bible, then, is examined not for the meaning or meanings proper to it, but for its ability to provide a pretext for philosophical doctrines external to it. Such an interpretive procedure thus takes as its starting point a truth external to the text and to which the text by means of interpretation will be made to conform. Such methods, according to Spinoza, are designed precisely to prevent a knowledge of the Scripture as it is, in its disorder and complexity.

Jehuda Alpakhar was a step closer to Spinoza in that he, unlike Maimonides, sought to "explain Scripture by Scripture". Just as Maimonides sought to reduce Scripture to a truth external to it, Alpakhar seeks to reduce external reality to the sole truth of the Scripture. But, as he argues that we "should accept as true or reject as false everything asserted or denied by Scripture", he must further argue "that Scripture never expresses asserts or denies anything which contradicted its assertions or negation elsewhere" (192). This leads Alpakhar to deny the very reality of the text, the diversity of its elements and the complexity of its history. He must conceal the fact that "scripture consists of different books, written at different times, to different people, by different authors" because his method requires it (192). All of his wisdom must be turned to the task of converting the literal text into metaphor in order thereby to create the appearance of linguistic and doctrinal harmony. While it is true that the meaning to which he reduces Scripture is internal to it, it is still only a fragment of the Scripture and its doctrines. Therefore his interpretations cast a shadow (the shadow of metaphor) over those parts of the Scripture that conflict with what is held to be its proper significance.

Spinoza's concept of interpretation marks a point of rupture with all prior theories by positing textual and doctrinal contradiction as irreducible and, as such, as indispensable signs of the historicity of the Scripture, the principle of intelligibility that allows us to explain the text as it is. The immense theoretical novelty of Spinoza's program can in part be measured by the reaction to the *Tractatus Theologico-Politicus* between 1670 (the date of the first anonymous edition) and 1700 (Vernière 1954). In England and in France the verdict was virtually unanimous: Spinoza, the "apostate Jew" as his less delicate critics were pleased to call him, was guilty of the most dangerous of crimes. He had severed Scripture from the living voice of God. It became, in the optic of his theory, mere matter to be examined like any other part of the natural world. Further, the examination to which he submitted the Bible revealed not the seamless perfection that was argued to be its most important, if hidden, property, but the joints and fractures that revealed its patchwork quality. The complexity of the Scripture was no longer the complexity of a mystery, of a hidden presence to be divined or deciphered by the initiated or the authorized, but rather an unexpectedly displayed complexity that the surface of the text clearly exhibited to anyone who did not willfully blind themselves to it. The very notion of a depth or a hidden dimension to the text is an attempt by interpreters to claim as intrinsic, doctrines that have in fact been added to the text. Scripture has no interior; it is pure externality.

The frightening vision of Scripture presented in the *Tractatus Theologico-Politicus* introduces a series of problems in the philosophical, theological and even literary reflection of the period. Among other things, Spinoza problematized the relation between a text and its author, a text and the world it supposedly represented. His critics saw in his utterances a subversion of the very notion of the authenticity of documents of any kind, even legal (Colie 1963, 204). But the age produced little in the way of sustained argument against Spinoza; the preferred mode of response to his work was denunciation. Shortly after the turn of the century, the tide of abuse receded and Spinoza was quietly buried. And yet it may well be that his mark upon the age has not been fully appreciated. For the revolutionary and unprecedented character of his work was only captured by philosophical and theological discourse *negatively*. A positive working out of his philosophy of interpretation to the extremity that it held out for itself was to occur in another region altogether: in a literary text that proclaimed its composite and heterogeneous character at the top of its voice; that exhibited its lapses and hiatuses for all to see; that, renouncing any claim to depth, reveled in the disorder of its own surface; that soberly contemplated its merely material nature as an object among other objects and that finally speculated on its own history – *A Tale of a Tub*.

The development of philosophy is a struggle whose history is written by its victors. The image of the age is often the dominant philosophical tendency's image of itself. However, if we turn to the defeated and disavowed minorities in thought we see that which the dominant tendency cannot itself see, that to which it remains necessarily blind. In particular, the unities that it presents (for example, rationalism, empiricism) appear, refracted though the discursive forces over which it dominates, fractured and unstable. We see the inconsistencies and conflicts internal to works and *oeuvres* themselves: Descartes preserves spiritual substance by marginalizing it; Spinoza, by declaring the presence of God equally in all things (*Deus sive Natura*), renders him absent rather than immanent; Hobbes, instead of upholding the authority of the Church by demonstrating the heterogeneity of Scripture, undermines it, opening the way to Spinoza's heresy *sans rivages*. The great interest of a work like Cudworth's *True Intellectual System* (the same might be said of More and Bentley) is that it shows the extent to which Anglican thought had internalized the doctrines it opposed and, in digesting them, decomposed them into their component elements, showing, in the process, their composite character.

In a fundamental sense, however, the Anglican critics of materialism remained external to the field they examined, to the extent that their works, while important, remained commentaries that evoked the norm of an attenuated scholasticism in their critique of Descartes, Gassendi, Hobbes and Spinoza. It was left to Swift in the realm of literary satire to develop the contradictions that an earlier generation of Anglican thinkers had carefully noted. It was in the realm of literature rather than philosophy that these contradictions could be set to work and played out as far as they would go. Swift's satire, as his most acute critic William Wotton noted, properly speaking has no norm. Swift inhabits the philosophies of his time to set them against themselves, to force them to the conclusions that their arguments pointed to but which they for the most part refused to, or could not, admit. It is not an exaggeration to say that it is only in the extremity of Swift's satire that a specific materialism (which is more a strategy than a doctrine) emerges. The effects of this strategy are satirically imagined because they cannot yet be rigorously thought out. If they are illustrated rather than demonstrated, it is because a concept like the materiality of speech, so central to *A Tale*, did not exist as a concept in 1700 but as the unthought and as yet unthinkable residue of a strain of seventeenth-century philosophy.

The three philosophical conflicts we have examined (the question of method, matter versus spirit, and the materiality of speech) are therefore in no sense external to the work, any more than the work is external to them. We are not speaking of influence, inspiration or even context (a word that in its very imprecision allows us to evade some of the most important questions of literary history). These conflicts are not models for the work to imitate. Rather, they erupt within the text as nodal points around which its diverse elements tend to converge. By studying these nodal points we may understand how the work is not simply historically determined but overdetermined, its disorder neither a fault nor the misapprehension of the uninitiated, but the material effect of its constitution.

3

A Tale of a Tub:
All is Meer Outside

As is well known, *A Tale of a Tub* consists of an allegory of the Reformation, interrupted by five digressions. The allegory is developed through the story of three bothers: Peter (who represents Catholicism), Martin (the Anglican Church) and Jack (dissenting Protestantism). The follies of Peter and Jack, described in some detail, only serve to highlight the wise moderation of Martin (of whom we are shown very little). The digressions address corruptions of learning by means of a narrator or narrators whose views we seem intended to reject (except at clearly underscored moments of ironic inversion). The religious allegory (Harth 1961) and the satire on learning (Starkman 1950) have been discussed at length by critics, as has the unity (whether formal or merely thematic) of the *Tale* as a whole (Paulson 1960; Clark 1970; Smith 1979).

In the light of the analysis presented in the previous chapter, however, it might prove productive to approach the work in a different way and pose the following question: how does the relation between matter and spirit, as it was problematized in the late seventeenth century, exist in the *Tale* not as a "theme", to which its diverse elements might be reduced, but, as we have argued, as a nodal point where diverse and conflicting meanings condense and combine? To answer this question, we will begin by describing a metaphorical set or series that traverses the *Tale*, to chart not simply the dispersion of its effects but, even more, the incompatibilities and antagonisms engendered by the particular group of metaphors in question. For the dispersion of effects through the work in no sense constitutes their neutralization (which would be another way of restoring harmony to the text). It is, rather, the very disposition of effects in conflict that we will describe and explain. Thus, while some critics have been willing to grant that Swift's satire is not univocal but may in fact be bivalent, its double-edged quality was seen as merely a more clever, economic and therefore efficient technique: killing two birds with one stone. Because we reject the hypothesis of textual unity guaranteed by authorial intention, we are forced to confront the polyvalent nature of certain of Swift's metaphors, the fact that they can and do serve more than one master.

The problem of matter and spirit recurs through the *Tale* without respect to the division of the work into the satire on abuses in learning and the satire on the abuses of religion (the allegory of the three brothers and the digressions). It is in the "Digression Concerning Madness" that the problem is most clearly exhibited *as a problem* and where the satire has proved, in its very polyvalence, in its multidirectionality, most elusive. Rather than attempt to establish whether it is Swift himself who speaks or a persona (or personae), we will attempt to identify the distinct philosophical positions that are to be found in the text and to examine the precise constellation they form. We will begin with a statement whose overdetermined philosophical character we noted earlier:

> For the Brain in its natural position and state of serenity, disposeth its owner to pass his life in the common forms without any Thought of subduing multitudes to his own power, his reasons or his visions and the more he shapes his understanding by the pattern of human learning, the less he is inclined to form parties after his particular notions, because that instructs him in his private infirmities, as well as in the stubborn ignorance of the people. (1958, 171)

The passage explains why, as the speaker argued in the preceding sentence, the "mighty revolutions that have happened in empire, in philosophy and in religion" must be the result of "a disturbance or transposition of the brain" (171), that is, madness. The statement thus seeks to define a norm against which the events in philosophy, empire and religion can be measured and judged abnormal or, in the language of the seventeenth century, unnatural. In fact, the statement, in however succinct a form, clearly seeks to re-establish a sense of the natural and the normal. The mind has a "natural position", a place and a purpose proper to it. The world as seen through the position indicated by this statement is the Anglican Aristotelian world in which nothing exists without a divinely ordained end. Further, the world glimpsed here is profoundly hierarchical. The dominance of the community over

87

the individual is not a triumph of culture over nature, as in Hobbes, for whom hierarchy is a hard-won victory over the anarchic egalitarianism proper to the state of nature. Rather, nature here is the source of order, a guarantee of "serenity". It is "natural" for individual reason to be subordinated to "the common forms" and "particular notions", to "the pattern of human learning". This edifying vision of community, hierarchy and tradition, however, is interrupted by the disjunctive intrusion of the next sentence: "But when a man's fancy gets astride on his reason, when imagination is at cuffs with the senses, and common understanding as well as common sense is kicked out of doors, the first proselyte he makes is himself; and when that is once compassed, the difficulty is not so great in bringing over others; a strong delusion always operating from without as vigorously as from within" (171). At first reading, the utterance appears consistent with that which precedes it. It seems merely to offer a comic account of what happens when the natural order of mental faculties is transposed, in contrast to the vision of order which it succeeds. And yet as we follow the concatenation of utterances in the text, we find that the sentence takes on other meanings. Evoked here is the natural arrangement of faculties, the disordering of which the sentence recounts: reason should dominate fancy, and, even more interestingly, imagination should at least be in harmony with (not "at cuffs with"), if not subordinate to, the senses, common sense and common understanding.

A positive satiric norm seems easily derived from the two utterances taken together (stated positively in the first sentence and negatively in the second). The natural hierarchy of the external world continues into the very heart and mind of man. A serenity is promised if obedience to the natural order is maintained. And yet a series of utterances follows which seems to disrupt and undercut the very possibility of such a normal world, and the comic disorder figured in the image of order overthrown foreshadows this disruption. It may be, the text will soon suggest, that if imagination is "at cuffs with the senses and common sense", the problem may inhere in the senses themselves. For, if serenity comes from the mind's acceptance of its natural position (and the complex of both internal and external, individual and social relations that such a position implies), opposing it is a happiness based on a rejection of this position.

Those entertainments and pleasures we most value in life are such as dupe and play wag with the senses. For if we take an examination of what is generally understood by happiness, as it has respect either to the understanding or the senses, we shall find all its properties and adjuncts will herd under this short definition, that it is a perpetual possession of being well deceived. (171)

The senses, which ought to provide material for the information of the understanding, seem themselves to seek what will "dupe and nag" them as that which is most conducive to happiness. The madness which leads to the brain's abandoning its natural position seems less a transposition or disturbance of the brain itself, as originally argued, than a disruption from without, abetted by the senses seeking happiness. But how can there be greater happiness in perpetual deception than in the acceptance of the mind's natural place? What is the relation between the edifying Aristotelianism of the earlier passage and the skeptical despair of the later? Let us try to explain this contradiction in terms of what the text itself offers and forego all recourse to what Swift "really thought". For this, one of the darkest passages in Swift's writings, only becomes darker as it proceeds. "And first with relation to the mind or understanding, 'tis manifest what mighty advantages fiction has over truth, and the reason is just at our elbow, because imagination can build nobler scenes and produce more wonderful revolutions than fortune or nature will be at expense to furnish" (171). Some critics have argued that the word "revolutions" signals that Swift is attacking the phantasmatic character of modern thought (Starkman 1950, 29–30). But this hardly exhausts the significance of the passage or limits its effects.

Swift sets into motion an opposition between appearance and reality (fiction versus. truth, imagination versus nature), which does not as yet necessarily contradict the Anglican Aristotelian doctrine exhibited earlier. For the general, the collective and the traditional incarnate truth, while the individual and the novel constitute mere fictions. Yet, in nominalist fashion, Swift raises questions about the ontological status of "fictions". He wonders whether "things imagined may not properly be said to exist as those that are seated in the memory" (1958, 172). An argument thus emerges from the constellation of statements: Because nature is fading, insipid and generally insufficient, happiness is based on appearances, delusions and fictions; but appearances themselves are real.

89

What is significant here is that the speaker does not mistake appearance for essence. On the contrary, he is fully aware of the distinction and rejects the essence of things:

> In the proportion that credulity is a more peaceful possession of the mind than curiosity; so far preferable is that wisdom which converses about the surface to that pretended philosophy which enters into the depth of things and then comes gravely back with informations and discoveries that in the inside they are good for nothing. (173)

This passage marks a dramatic reversal: it is not simply that modern philosophy has turned away from the depths, from the search for true natures, essences and final causes; it is that in its curiosity, its probing, it has shown that the interior is "good for nothing". The success of the passage's irony depends on its capacity constantly to evoke two senses of "interior": (i) the physical or corporeal, and (ii) the spiritual or incorporeal. No matter how carefully we dissect the body, how deeply we penetrate, we will not find anything like soul or consciousness (not even in the pineal gland!). Nothing is more tenuous in this section than the idea of spirit or soul. In fact, Swift attacks knowledge derived only from the senses, which "never examine farther than the colour, the shape, the size and whatever other qualities dwell or are drawn by art upon the outward of the bodies" (173) or from reason "with tools for cutting and opening and mangling and piercing, offering to demonstrate that they are not of the same consistence quite through" (173). In one sense, Swift criticizes the modern tendency to formulate a method that will redirect knowledge away from ends, purposes, natures and essences, to surfaces (as if of solid bodies). Indeed, Cudworth criticized the Cartesian position that the ultimate ends and final causes of this world could not be known, and argued that the incorporeal essences of things are what knowledge must seek. But the Anglican position is not even to be found in Swift's text.

Nowhere in *A Tale* is the complexity of the history of ideas, its character as a struggle, placed so clearly in relief as in this section from the "Digression Concerning Madness". Nowhere can we see with such clarity the impossibility of Swift's ideological position, and correspondingly the necessity of his entering the enemy camp itself to exploit its internal conflicts and antagonisms. It makes little sense to speak of a persona here, given the rapid succession of divergent doctrines exhibited in the text. Nor does it seem par-

ticularly useful to establish a plurality of personae. The text is a
patchwork of utterances, taken from the discursive ensembles
described in the previous chapter, but arranged in a manner whose
specificity makes them irreducible to their "origins". It is perhaps
more accurate to speak of theoretical positions and constructions
than of personae or voices. Rather than conceiving of the text as
composed of a series of personae, each of which ironically condemns itself at the same moment that it ridicules the other equally
noxious personae, we ought perhaps to speak of a playing of philosophical positions against each other in the absence of a secure
theoretical terrain to defend, of a setting of one construction
against another: Spinoza against Descartes and Gassendi.

Thus Swift abandons the Aristotelian position stated at the
outset of the section, to infiltrate materialist positions and subvert
them from within. This tactic itself is a comment on the lapsed
character of the Anglican position, which is no more than an
abandoned edifice. It can no longer seriously oppose the forces
that have already ravaged it and left it defenseless. Of course, a
systematic objective is immanent in the strategy of inhabiting a
series of philosophical positions. That is not to say, however, that
the strategy does or even could succeed, that Swift does not, as
William Wotton charged, demolish the very position he seeks to
defend. There is a terrible miscalculation of forces: the satiric
attack on the inconsistencies of Gassendi, Descartes and Hobbes
– the exploitation of the incompatibility of the components of
which their doctrines are composed, of the tensions internal to
them – opens the way not to the invalidated Aristotelianism of
orthodox Anglicanism but to the consistent materialism or anti-
transcendentalism of Spinoza.

Thus Gassendi's pronouncement that knowledge of appearances
or surfaces is itself the only true knowledge, which in some way
is meant to protect incorporeal final causes and essences, to make
them "off limits" to the new rationality that had emerged in the
seventeenth century, is revealed in Swift's text to have had a second opposed (and, from the outset, disavowed) objective: the destruction of essences, the constitution of a world of surfaces without
depth. Such a reading of Gassendi (which was far from uncommon
in the seventeenth century) is in turn made more plausible to the
extent that it intersects in the "Digression Concerning Madness"
with Spinoza's reading of Descartes. Spinoza set Descartes against
himself, taking his philosophy at its word despite the denials and

defenses that traverse it. For Spinoza banished not simply the ghost from the machine but all prior order from the machine itself by systematically disengaging every hypothesis of transcendence (and in this he went far beyond Hobbes) from the world. Swift's text succeeds in identifying a strategy immanent in a series of philosophical works of the seventeenth century, a strategy that is nowhere explicitly formulated (not even by Spinoza) and which can be grasped only in the denials, disavowals and inconsistencies that are its symptomatic expressions. It is only through the operation of Swift's satire that this strategy emerges as such in its clarity. Few if any writers of the time shared Swift's ability to inhabit philosophical positions and to make them speak in their own voice, grasping from within the defenses by which they attempted to make themselves deaf and blind to the actual effects they produced.

It is thus that the world described in the "Digression Concerning Madness" is brought into focus: a solely material world without transcendence, a world ruled not even by mechanical, physical laws but characterized by an infinite productivity without origin or end. In this Swift undoubtedly triumphs: he has made the philosophy of his time speak its truth. But the moment of truth, Swift's very triumph, marks his utter ruin or rather the ruin of the position he seeks to defend. For the truth he has uncovered proves, as one critic put it, "all too convincing" (Empson 1935, 60), and the work is conducted by the force of its own arguments (the ironic effect of which persistently fades) to the "serenity" of "being a fool among knaves". In relation to a world without spirit or transcendence, a world of solid surfaces without depth, the notions of an incorporeal deity, an ordered cosmos, a soul, are themselves the illusions and fictions that disguise and hide a merely material world. Far from being hidden beneath or beyond the world, they are an artificial and purely external addition to it. Many of Swift's contemporaries saw clearly, as William Wotton did, that Swift's satire returns against itself and demolishes the very position from which the attack was launched. Swift had succeeded precisely in making visible and palpable what the age had only been able to contemplate negatively.

The passage from the "Digression Concerning Madness", so complex in itself, is illustrated or figured in Section II of A Tale, whose meanings it allows us to grasp. The truth of which the allegory of the coats and the account of the tailor-worshippers are figurations is distilled into a single strange note that Swift added to the 1720 edition of *A Tale* (Part I of his *Miscellaneous Works, Comical and Diverting*): "*Omnia Vanitas* all is meer outside". Once again Swift arrives, impelled by the very force of his imagery and its arrangement, at unthinkable truths: the primacy of appearances and surface, the exteriority of essence, the artificiality and, even at the extreme, the historicity of human institutions. In particular, it is necessary to examine the ways in which the apparent simplicity, directness and innocence of the allegory of the coats is complicated and invested with different, even opposed, meanings by the account of tailor-worship.

At the very outset the coat as metaphor inaugurates a series of complications and conflicts. The allegory begins: "Sons, because I have purchased no Estate nor was born to any I have long considered some good legacies to bequeath you; and at last with much care as well as expense have provided each of you (here they are) a new coat" (1958, 73). At this point Swift added, as a note to the fifth edition of *A Tale*, Wotton's interpretation of the coats as "the garments of the Israelites" (73). Then, a comment attributed to a certain Lambin is appended to the note, refuting it. "An error (with submission) of the learned commentator; for by the Coats are meant the doctrine and faith of Christianity, by the wisdom of the divine founder fitted to all times, places and circumstances" (73).

Beyond the fact that Swift chose to supply the meaning of his own figure (a point that will be taken up in detail later), the passage and the notes appended to it allow us to see that the metaphor produces conflicting effects, and that at the heart of the conflict is the opposition of matter and spirit, the unruliness of which plays havoc with the order of the text and its meaning. For the choice of "coat" to represent "the doctrine and faith of Christianity" is attended with numerous inescapable risks, especially given the central obsessions and fears of *A Tale*. The figuration of the abstract by the concrete (doctrine and faith are represented as coats) is not itself necessarily problematic; such allegorizings are a commonplace of the rhetoric of the sermon. The choice of "coat", however, is overdetermined. The metaphor allows Swift to posit both the eternal utility and the eternal validity of Christianity: "These coats have two virtues contained in them: One is, that with good wearing, they will last you fresh and sound as long as you live. The other is that they will grow in the same proportion with your bodies, lengthening and widening of themselves as to be

93

always fit" (73). But the divergence between Wotton's interpretation and Swift's professed meaning is instructive.

Wotton, who was generally an acute interpreter of *A Tale*, was uncharacteristically literal in his interpretation of the coats, unable to grant to the metaphor the breadth of meaning that Swift intended it to support. The concentration that the text brings to bear upon itself at this point (with its notes upon notes) is symptomatic: it is an attempt to forestall the very constellation of meaning that develops around coats and clothing in general. For a fatal necessity puts Swift at odds with himself, with his own stated intentions, and impels him to undermine the particular metaphorical function that he seeks to enforce. The very qualities that make the coat a fitting vehicle in the ironic development of *A Tale*, its attack on dissenting Protestantism as well as Catholicism, tend to return, as Wotton noted in his commentary, against Christianity *tout court*. And our discussion of the "Digression on Madness" allows us to see why. A work that is intended to defend the notions of spirit and soul, of an incorporeal deity, from the materialisms of the day, allegorizes Christianity as a coat only at great peril: the coat itself is artificially fabricated (in contrast to the natural growth of the body it covers) and is external, a covering that both protects and conceals. Further, as if the danger of such interpretations were not great enough, Swift fully and openly exploits these meanings, interrupting the allegory with the account of the clothes worshippers. The effect of this digressive "satyr upon Dress and Fashion", which is supposed to strengthen the ironic assault on the Papists' and Dissenters' perversion of true doctrine by means of the metaphorical device of the coats, is profoundly to subvert the intended effect of section II, the allegory of the coats in general. Thus Wotton follows the logic of the satire to its conclusion and notes the spectacular failure of its irony.

> All this sir, I own to be true: but then I would not so shoot at an enemy, as to hurt myself at the same time. The foundation of the doctrines of the church of England is right and came from God: Upon this the Pope and councils called and confirmed by then, have built, as St. Paul speaks Hay and Stubble, perishable and slight materials, which when they are once consumed, that the foundations may appear, then we shall see what is faulty, and what is not. But our *Tale-Teller* strikes at the very root. *'Tis all* with him a *farce and all* a ladle, as a very facetious poet says upon another occasion. (1705, 321–2)

In a certain sense, the metaphor of clothes (and of coats) returns upon and undoes itself insofar as it served as a vehicle to figure both true religion and its perversions, positing in the very complexity of its effects a world without spirit.

Phillip Harth has identified the passage in which Swift describes the clothes worshippers' "system of belief" as a parody of the opening of the introduction to *Leviathan* (Harth 1961, 83–5). It remains for us to examine the parody itself as a relation between two utterances or groups of utterances, to determine how and to what extent Swift transforms Hobbes in the process of parody. Further, we should note in what way something of Hobbes passes into the text of *A Tale*, producing effects which may or may not conform to its general project, that is, which may either strengthen the ironic assault on materialism or weaken it, and by weakening it turn the assault against itself. *Leviathan* begins:

> Nature (The art whereby God hath made and governs the world) is by the art of man, as in many other things, so in this also imitated, that it can make an artificial animal. For seeing life is but a motion of the limbs, the beginning whereof is in some principal part within; why may we not say, that all automata (engines that move themselves by springs and wheels as doth a watch) have an artificial life? For what is the Heart but a spring and the nerves but so many strings and the joynts but so many wheels giving motion to the whole body, such as was intended by the artificer? Art goes yet further imitating that rational and most excellent work and nature, Man. For by art is created that great Leviathan the common-wealth or state (in Latin *Civitas*) which is but an artificial man; though of greater stature and strength than the natural for whose protection and defence it was intended; and in which the sovereign is an artificial soul, as giving life and motion to the whole body; the magistrates and other officers of Judicature and Execution, artificial joynts; rewards and punishment (by which fastened to the state of the sovereignty, every joynt and member is moved to perform his duty) are the nerves that do the same in the body natural. (1968, 81)

Before we confront Hobbes's passage with its parodic double, noting beyond the effects of the rhetoric proper to parody (for example, hyperbole, catachresis etc.) the meanings engendered by the parodic transformation which precisely differentiate it from its object, we must note certain features of the original.

First, according to Harth, "in this paragraph Hobbes is of course simply developing an elaborate analogy of part to part and whole to whole" (1961, 83–5). While it is true that Hobbes has constructed an analogy between the human body and the social body (the commonwealth), the effects produced by this analogy are in no sense contained by its rhetorical simplicity. For, taken in isolation, the comparison of the body to the commonwealth can be found in Aristotle's *Politics*. It was a common feature of Medieval political reasoning and persisted well beyond the seventeenth century. How, therefore, do we account for the scandal that this passage raised at the moment of its appearance?

Second, the first two sentences of Hobbes's introduction, omitted in Harth's excerpt, are crucial for understanding the offensive character of the passage. In fact, these utterances display, in a condensed form, a number of Hobbes's most disturbing theses. Nature is immediately qualified by the following parenthetical phrase: "The art whereby God hath made and governs the world." This phrase is not so much a definition as a deliberate redefinition, according to which Nature is precisely that which has traditionally been held to be its opposite: art. The distinction between nature and art (*physis* and *techne* for the Greeks) was essential to political theories that distinguished between political forms or particular regimes that are in accordance with a prior (divine) order and those which violate this order. To speak of nature as God's *art* is to devalue it, to overturn its primacy over culture. The statement effects a collapse of the divine into the human, and the natural into the artificial. Thus, the notion that nature is that art whereby God "governs the world" radically alters the meaning of nature and natural law. The goal of politics is no longer to imitate nature (as an expression of God) but to contain it, shape it; to suspend its violence and ameliorate its poverty. Nature is thus defined at the outset as that which must be overcome and eliminated from human society. Civil war is nothing less than the state of nature in its anarchic purity.

Third, the comparison of the human body to a machine, instead of annexing machines to nature, renders nature itself a machine. As such it no longer can be said to express the essence of its creator, who is as independent of what he has created as man is of his creation: they are distinct corporeal existences. It is not that art and technology are infused with an incorporeal divine spirit; it is rather that Hobbes has forced an evacuation of spirit from the material world. He effected a "corporealisation of substance", as one commentator put it (Spragens 1973). There is no ghost in

Hobbes's machine: "And therefore if a man should talk to me of ... immaterial substances ... I should not say that he were in error but that his words were without meaning; that is to say Absurd" (1968, 113).

Let us now confront Hobbes with the text of Swift's parody, the statement of the tailor-worshippers' system of belief:

> They held the universe to be a large suit of clothes, which invest every-
> thing: that the earth is invested by the air; the air is invested by the
> stars; and the stars are invested by the primum mobile. Look on this
> globe of earth, you will find it to be a very complete and fashionable
> dress. What is that which some call land, but a fine coat faced with
> green? Or the sea, but a waistcoat of water-tabby. Proceed to the par-
> ticular works of the creation, you will find how curious journeyman
> nature hath been to trim up the vegetable beaux; observe how sparkish
> a periwig adorning the head of a beech and what a fine doublet of
> white satin is worn by the birch. To conclude from all, what is man
> himself but a microcoat or rather a complete suit of clothes with all its
> trimmings. As for his body, there is no dispute; but examine even the
> acquirements of his mind, you will find them all contribute in their
> order towards furnishing out an exact dress. To instance no more: is
> not religion a cloak; honesty a pair of gloves worn out in the dirt; self
> love a surtout; vanity a shirt; and conscience a pair of breeches; which,
> though a cover for lewdness as well as nastiness, is easily slipt down for
> the service of both? (1958, 78)

The most obvious characteristic of the passage is that, in contrast to Hobbes's play of the artificial against the natural, Swift sets the external against the internal. In fact, the passage systematically abolishes the very notion of interiority, playing the literal material meaning of a word like "invest" against its metaphorical, imma-terial sense. The first assertion, that the universe is "a large suit of clothes", is certainly, as Harth argues, a pushing of Hobbes's mechanist metaphor for nature to an extreme. It is not, however, that Swift's passage is more reductive than Hobbes's; it is that the particular reduction to mechanism was current in the seventeenth century. The metaphor of clothes captures certain of the key fea-tures of the mechanist metaphor, while evading its positive conno-tations, its legitimacy as a working scientific notion. The verb "invest" in the opening of the passage is in effect a substitute for a concept like the Neo-Platonic "expression", which posits the cosmos as a hierarchy of levels of expression of God's essence. In Swift's text, however, the term "invests" oscillates between a spiritual sense (the *primum mobile* invested in nature) and a material sense (that the different parts of the cosmos are enclosed, covered, a group of strata irreducible to one another). The sentence as a whole thus produces a singular effect: it allows us to see, by the very ingenuity of the parody, the possibility of a thoroughly materialist interpretation of a traditional spiritual motif: creation as expression, the presence or immanence of God in all the phenomena of the world He has made. It is perhaps for this reason that the next sentence abandons the disturbing equivocation on the term "investment", to reduce the complexity of the satire: "Look on this globe of earth, you will find it to be a very complete and fashionable dress" (78). The retreat, however, lasts only a few sentences, and Swift inescapably is led by the very polyvalence of the materials with which he has chosen to work to formulate some of the most disturbing utterances in his entire *oeuvre*.

"What is man himself but a microcoat or rather a complete suit of clothes with all its trimmings" (78). Here Swift obviously alludes to Hobbes's vision of the human body as a kind of automaton, and yet typically the irony of the allusion does not exhaust the meaning of the statement. For apart from marking a substitution of the sartorial for the (scientifically valid) mechanical metaphor in order to emphasize its artificiality, the idea of man as a suit of clothes pushes to their fulfillment the very implications of mechanistic thought from which thinkers like Descartes and Hobbes turned away. It is precisely to the development of these possibilities that Swift is led by the logic of his irony. The mechanistic appropriation of the notion of the microcosm deprived it of its spiritual sense, of the resemblance that bound man to the world whose totality he represented in miniature. For if the world was the expression of God's essence and man expressed the world, then man also expressed the essence of God. The mechanistic philosophy of the seventeenth century deprived man's resemblance to the world of any spiritual significance, for the machine in no way resembled its mechanic, to whose essence it remained radically external. Man's resemblance to nature, his microcosmic qualities, were henceforth a source of anxiety rather than comfort, a sign of the abyss that separated him from God.

Accordingly, Swift's satire turns from the body to the mind and the soul, moving from the exterior to the interior in search of that incorporeal, immaterial element contained in the envelope of the corporeal. Solid bodies, however, have no interior. Those operations, mental and intellectual, that were traditionally conceived as incorporeal and spiritual could be rewritten as external and material existence. Swift undoubtedly seeks ironically to undermine Spinozist anti-psychologism: "As to his body there can be no dispute but examine even the requirements of his mind, you will find them all contribute in their order towards furnishing out an exact dress" (78). Suddenly, however, the use of clothes as a device to ridicule the abolition of immaterial substance and of interiority returns against the irony itself. It is not simply that the irony fails or, as we noted in an earlier passage, fades. Rather, the ironic use of clothes as a metaphoric substitute for mechanism works by doubling upon itself: "is not religion a cloak; honesty a pair of gloves worn out in the dirt; self love a surtout; vanity a shirt; and conscience a pair of breeches; which though a cover for lewdness as well as nastiness, is easily slipt down for the service of both?" (78).

Wotton's commentary immediately establishes an association of meanings and effects that modern critics have for the most part refused to see. "Religion a cloak", by virtue of its appearance in the account of tailor worship, introduces a fatal complexity in the allegory of the coats. The adequacy of "coat" as a figuration of true religion is called radically into question by the mere appearance of this phrase. Further, "religion" is anomalous in the series to which it belongs in the text (that is, the qualities of the mind: honesty, self-love, vanity and conscience). It is not an internal mental property satirically rewritten as artificial, material and external; it is superfluous in this passage, unnecessary to the satiric project. As a superfluous element, however, it is not simply neutralized in the action of the satire. On the contrary, it enters into this action to modify its effects. The presence of religion in this series turns the irony of the passage against the allegory of the coats, depriving the very figure of the coat of any positive valence. The reader is thereby conducted to the proposition immanent in the effects of Swift's satire, a proposition no less true for being disavowed in the Apology: religion in a world of matter without spirit is *artificial*, a purely human practice, and it is *material*; it is nothing more than the rituals, practices and institutions that compose it. No transcendent spirit or logos underlies (or is immanent within) it as a guarantee of its authenticity and "naturality". An officer of the Church, a bishop is therefore no less artificial and material than the "apt conjunction of lawn and black satin" that signify his authority.

It is thus not the truth of the Holy Spirit that is the foundation of religious rituals, practices and institutions and that is expressed in them. Quite the contrary: it is the rituals, practices and institutions in their materiality that *produce* the "spiritual" truths that appear to be their foundation but which are in fact their excrescence, a cover and a camouflage that conceal their merely material nature. Althusser has noted a similar inversion of the order of things in Pascal's *Pensées*:

> Pascal says more or less: 'Kneel down, move your lips in prayer, and you will believe'. He thus scandalously inverts the order of things, bringing like Christ, not peace but strife, and in addition something hardly Christian (for woe to him who brings scandal into the world!) – scandal itself. A fortunate scandal which makes him stick with Jansenist defiance to a language that directly names the reality. (Althusser 1971, 168).

At this point the political stakes of *A Tale of a Tub*, its relation to Swift's stated positions, become clear. The problematization of spirit, the disappearance of transcendentality, the abolition of immutable essences, all render imperative the defense of the rituals, practices and institutions of the Church, its visible and actual manifestations, as something like necessary fictions, beautiful lies that conceal an abominable truth. Swift's consistently High Church politics are thus a consequence of and a response to, not a rejection of, the problematization of spirit that traversed the philosophies of the seventeenth century. Hobbes (whose religious politics Swift shared) justified a state Church and official doctrine (including mandatory conformity) with the argument that because we cannot *know* individually the will and dictates of God, that is, because the realm of spirit was unknowable, the sovereign and his laws must be regarded as legitimate authorities in matters of faith. Swift's satire, by the action of its metaphors, conducts us to an even more extreme position. The absence of transcendental and immutable truths must itself be concealed by the cloak of religion (reduced itself to institutional materiality), which in turn having once been fixed (and what could be more tenuous and questionable than the "original legitimacy" of the Anglican church?) must be forever defended against all attempts to weaken it in the name of religious tolerance or freedom of conscience. The more that religious, scientific and philosophical discourses tended to call into question the natural and divinely appointed character of the

Church or State, the greater the need to protect their very form and appearance. Thus, especially important were laws like the Test Act (enforcing occasional conformity to Church ritual, the taking of communion and so on), which emphasized the appearance of faith, the act itself, irrespective of the intentions or feelings of the occasional conformist. Swift's very conservatism, like Pascal's, betrays a fear that, to use the language of the *Argument Against Abolishing Christianity*, Christianity is nominal not real, its truth a surface truth, a material truth. The ironic assault on the problematizations of spirit does not so much fail or falter as succeed too well.

But if "all is meer outside", the interiority of man does not disappear altogether. While every operation of the understanding, every passion, may be seen as material, and the very conceptualization that permits their being "inside" called radically into question, the text persistently preserves a space that may be called an inside or an interior. This space once contained that which was deemed essential and proper to man as opposed to the accidental and inessential body in which it was housed. For a thinker like Pascal (whose convergence with Swift at certain points we have already noted), the space within man was as infinitely empty as the silent space without. The interiority of man was an abyss, an indelible mark of God's abandonment of the world. Such notions, however, are not to be found in Swift's work: it is full space not empty space that frightens him. *A Tale* itself is as crowded and dense as the world it depicts. If the inside of man, deprived of the possibility of immateriality or incorporeality, mirrors the full world without, what images does it present to us? Or, to return to the system of the clothes-worshippers, what is hidden and concealed under the "celestial suit", the "outward clothing" of the soul?

> Others of these professors, though agreeing in the main system were yet more refined upon certain branches of it; and held that man was an animal of two dresses, the natural and celestial suit, which were the body and the soul: That the soul was the outward and the body the inward clothing; that the latter was *ex traduce*; but the former of daily creation and circumfusion. This last they proved by scripture, because in them we live and move and have our being; as likewise by philosophy, because they are all in all and all in every part. Besides, said they, separate these two and you will find the body to be only a senseless unsavory carcass. By all which it is manifest that the outward dress must needs be the soul. (79–80)

The phrase "all in all and all in every part" set in the apparatus of the clothes-philosophy is deprived of all spiritual significance. The very possibility of a spirit "indwelling" is excluded. The soul and body are material existences external to one another, their relation is one of exteriority: the soul is woven around the body. But Swift's ironic reversal of the priority of the soul over the body, his rendering of everything spiritual material, his systematic abolition of immaterial interiority in the service of his satire (all of which, as we have seen, are the outcome of a strategic intensification and acceleration of the general problematization of spirit at certain key points) impel the narrative of the satire toward the evocation of an overwhelming disgust. For while Cudworth speaks of the modern species of madness, pneumatophobia, the fear of spirit, Swift's text exhibits precisely the opposite disposition: hylophobia, a fear and hatred of matter.

It is in section VIII, the account of Aeolism, that the abolition of spirit is most thorough and the disgust that this abolition evokes most apparent. The ruthless systematizing of Swift's elimination of immaterial substance from the world is no doubt an effect of the complexity of the play of metaphors and of theoretical positions. It is this section that Wotton found most consistently offensive, and it is not difficult to see why. Swift's irony is turned against nothing less than inspiration itself, in an attack that seems calculated to demolish the Dissenters' celebration of spiritual enthusiasm while preserving intact the spiritual foundations of true religion. But Swift miscalculated: at no point in *A Tale* does the movement of the satire, the multiplication of metaphoric effects, the reciprocal reaction of these effects upon each other, force Swift to deviate so strongly from the project that forms the basis of the work. As Wotton argued, the "game of leap-frog between the flesh and the spirit" by which Swift attempts to strike at one sect of Christianity manages rather "to wound the whole by that means" (1705, 326). Wotton concludes that *A Tale* "is one of the prophanest Banters upon the religion of Jesus Christ, as such, that ever yet appeared" (324). It remains for us to trace that "game at leap-frog between the flesh and spirit" as it plays through the account of Aeolism, finally effacing the distinction between matter and spirit.

> The learned Aeolists maintain the original cause of all things to be wind, from which principle this whole universe was at first produced and into which it must at last be resolved.... This is what the *Adepti*

understand by their *Anima Mundi*; that is to say, the spirit, or breath or wind of the world. For examine the whole system by the particulars of nature and you will find it not to be disputed. For, whether you please to call the forma informans of Man by the name of *Siritus, Animus, Afflatus* or *Anima*; what are all these but several appellations for wind? (324)

Let us first remark that several notes are appended to the word "Aeolists", each of which signals that "all those that pretend to inspiration" have come under attack. Aeolism is Jack's system, the system of Protestant Dissent (Starkman 1950, 49–57). Since Puritanism is one of the two "abuses of religion" satirized in *A Tale*, there is nothing particularly surprising about Swift's ridicule of enthusiasm. The materials brought to bear in the attack, however, are surprising. From the very outset he contests the Dissenters' claims to spirituality, not by invoking a positive norm of religious inspiration against which we might measure the abuses of the more extreme Protestant sects, but by subverting the very notion of spirit. In the process a number of distinct philosophical positions are arrayed against each other. First, as a number of critics have noted, Swift deploys "inspiration" as a linchpin to connect dissenting enthusiasm to the (discredited) spiritual occultisms of Paracelsus and Thomas Vaughn (1958, 49–57). The seeming omnipresence of the spirit of the Lord to the Puritans is made to resemble the occultist notion of an *anima mundi*.

As if the aggregation of enthusiasm and occultism were not enough to condemn Puritanism, Swift cannot resist the temptation to overdetermine the attack, to force the metaphor of Aeolism into the field against still another enemy. For the question that concludes the passage cited above, "what are *"Spiritus, Animus, Afflatus* or *Anima* ... but several appellations for wind?", cannot fail to recall the rhetoric and method of Hobbes's *Leviathan*. Swift returns to the introduction to Leviathan to parody it again as he did in section II of the *Tale* ("For what is the heart but a spring..."), but adding to it a parody of *Leviathan* Chapter 34, "Of the Signification of Spirit, Angel, Inspiration in the Books of the Holy Scripture", In this chapter Hobbes sets out to reconcile scripture with the primary assertion that "the universe, being the aggregate of all Bodies, there is no real part thereof that is not also body; nor any thing properly a body that is not also a part of (that aggregate of all bodies) the universe" (Hobbes 1968, 428). To do so he must redefine spirit, angel and inspiration as corporeal entities. Accordingly, we are told that "the proper signification of spirit in common speech is either a subtle, fluid and invisible Body, or a Ghost or other Idol or phantasm of the Imagination" (429–30). To put it plainly, "to say an angel or Spirit is (in that sense) an incorporeal substance, is to say that there is no angel or spirit at all" (439). The spirit of God in the Scripture often means no more than "a wind or breath", as in the phrase from Genesis, "the spirit of God moved upon the face of the waters". From the foregoing, Hobbes concludes that the term inspiration taken in its proper sense "is nothing but the blowing into a man some thin and subtle air or wind, in such a manner as a man filleth a bladder with his breath" (440). The only other use of inspiration is metaphorical: a setting into motion of some causal relation between bodies.

We begin now to see the complexity proper to the account of Aeolism – the condensation of Puritanism, occultism and corporeal materialism into a single motif – the economy of which is remarkable. Swift sets three "subversive" doctrines against each other, hoping to kill three birds with one stone. If we leave it at that, however, taking Swift at his word as most critics have done, we have reduced the work to the intention that can be discerned within it. The scandal of this section of *A Tale*, the horror that it inspired in Swift's contemporaries, becomes merely a mistake, the unfortunate effect of a collective misreading. Simply to state Swift's intention or to note in passing the agility or virtuosity of three-way satire is inadequate. For in no other section of *A Tale* does the work so systematically betray (in both senses of the word) its intention and diverge so fundamentally from its satiric project. In particular, we must answer the following question: what are the effects (as they are inscribed in the text) of this setting of positions and doctrines against each other?

The identification of Puritanism and occultism (whether at the expense of the former or the latter) does not at first appear particularly problematic. Phillip Harth has demonstrated the existence of such argumentation in the work of Anglican theologians such as Henry More and Joseph Glanvill (1961, 59–64). But More was careful to define enthusiasm as the "misconceit of being inspired", in order to differentiate true from false inspiration (More 1656). In contrast, Swift tells us in no fewer than three notes that his satire is directed against "all pretenders to inspiration whatsoever". By what paradox does Swift, in a work that attacks the materialism of Descartes, Gassendi, Hobbes and Spinoza, turn against the overestimation of spirit, against notions of its presence in all things as *anima mundi?* For although it was a concept central to certain forms of occultism, the concept of *anima mundi* was of ancient lineage and as such treated with respect by Cudworth and More (Cudworth 1845, Vol. 3, 407). If anything, it was the rational kernel of occultism, the least objectionable part of its doctrine. Harth, discussing Swift's attack on the formulas *"ex traduce"* and "all in all and all in every part" in section II, allows us to begin to answer this question. Citing Glanvill and More, he demonstrates that these ideas "had come under attack during the Restoration era" for lending support to materialism (1961, 82–3).

The notion of *anima mundi* had become a weapon in the arsenal of materialism – in fact, one of its most cunning ruses. For unlike the mechanism of Descartes and Hobbes and the atomism of Gassendi, Spinoza's road to atheism began in the shadowy world of Neo-Platonism. Gilles Deleuze in particular has described the way that Neo-Platonist theories of the word as the expression of God or an emanation from God tended, as they were taken up by Christian thinkers in the late Middle Ages and the Renaissance, to complicate rather than solve the problems and questions that arose concerning the idea of creation (1990, 153–69). We have already shown how in Spinoza's hands the seemingly innocuous and even orthodox formula of "all in all and all in every part" was rewritten *"Deus sive Natura"*, positing an exact coincidence of the Deity and his creation. The result of this operation was of course not lost on the orthodox of the time, who saw in Spinoza's version of "God is in all things and all things are in God" the disappearance of God into things. God the immanent cause became God the absent cause whose absence left not a single trace in a full world. Puritan enthusiasm and occultist pantheism merge in Swift's text insofar as they posit an excess of spirit; spirit taken beyond its proper bounds invades and mingles promiscuously with bodies and things, finally becoming, in the vertigo of enthusiasm or hermetic zeal, indistinguishable from the matter that must be its contrary. Thus the movement of Swift's satire reproduces the movement of the spiritualist and pantheist tendencies of his time, imitating Spinoza's "God or Nature" in its definition of the *anima mundi* as "the spirit or breath or wind of the world". Spirit disappears into its material expression.

We may now begin to see that the playing of positions against each other is not the result of an artistic choice, a deliberate playful display of virtuosity and the mastery of irony, but a necessity virtually forced on Swift by the very nature of his project. To attack enthusiasm and extreme spiritualism directly in an age when Hobbes could declare that the very notion of incorporeal being was mere nonsense was very risky indeed. It was not uncommon for serious Anglican thinkers (for example, More and Glanvill) in the second half of the seventeenth century to feel compelled to defend the existence of ghosts as proof of spiritual existence. Swift must therefore establish in the course of his satire on enthusiasm that the spiritualism of the age, the renewed interest in inspiration, was not spiritual at all, but a question of material (mechanical, corporeal) operations "clothed" in the garb of spirit. For this task, an arsenal of arguments and demonstrations was at hand, thoughtfully provided by Hobbes and Spinoza. Thus, what the enthusiasts or occultists worshiped as spirit, what they felt as inspiration, the miracles and supernatural events they celebrated, were in fact no more than movements of "subtle bodies" that, if they were properly examined, could be explained by the laws and regular operations and actions of nature. The force of the materialist arguments is so great that, far from using them for his own purposes, Swift is rather used by them. When he goes so far as to give an entirely corporeal account (heavily weighted towards the sexual and the scatological) of the religious sentiments of the Dissenters, Swift makes no attempt to limit the jurisdiction of this kind of argument. The text, in fact, offers little that would permit a defense of Swift's own faith from such charges. Swift employs "materials" (philosophical and theological argument) that are not of his own making. Compounded and combined, even in the "controlled environment" of literary satire, they proved combustible or even explosive. In a word, Swift, by combining spiritualism and materialism, played with fire. Section VIII of *A Tale* is a conflagration in which true religion is consumed along with the false. In the end only a material residue is left.

It must be understood, however, that this tragic misalliance, this tragic miscalculation of forces, is not an individual "error" on the part of Swift, an error to be explained by his atheism or by his psychopathology. It is rather a symptom of the conflict of forces internal to the field of philosophy in Swift's time. Phillip Harth has shown that Swift's maneuver in this section of *A Tale* was typical of Anglican arguments against enthusiasm and occultism. However, we must go on to note the difficulties and problems of this general strategy. As we saw earlier, the Anglican intelligentsia (the Cambridge Platonists, the Boyle lecturers) had ceded so much theoretical ground to their materialist adversaries that they had difficulty distinguishing their own positions from those they opposed. They preferred to turn the enemy's batteries against him, as Bentley put it. But to turn the enemy's batteries against one's co-religionists was another matter altogether. Henry More's deployment of materialist arguments and metaphors is highly symptomatic: his work, in its development, is fundamentally a reaction to itself or to those elements of mechanistic or atomistic thought grafted on to it in operations that were not always successful. In his work *The Immortality of the Soul* (1662), we see a disposition of arguments very similar to that found in section VIII of the *Tale*. More's purpose is to prove beyond a reasonable doubt the existence of incorporeal essence in the world in the wake of Hobbes's *Leviathan* (1651). In doing so, More employs a strategy that is similar to that of Swift, a setting of positions against each other, and with results that are just as questionable.

In order to defend spirit and soul, More is forced at certain points to differentiate his views not simply from those of Hobbes or Lucretius but also from those which posit an excess of spirit. The fact that More had compared Puritanism and occultism in his earlier *Enthusiasmus Triumphatus* (1656) and, as Harth has established (1961, 78–80), saw both as potentially related to atheism, makes the logic of the following passage in which More seeks to prove against Paracelsus that the sun and the stars are not spiritual presences even more significant:

> That the light is a very glorious thing, and the lustre of the stars very lovely to look upon, and that the body of the sun is to full of splendour and majesty, that without flattery, we may profess ourselves constrained to look aside as not being able to bear the brightness of his aspect; all this must be acknowledged for truth: but that these are so many eyes of heaven and watch over the earth, so many kind and careful spectators and intermeddlers also in human affairs as that fanciful chemist Paracelsus conceits ... this I must confess I am not so paganly superstitious to believe one syllable of; but think it may be demonstrated to be a mere fancy, especially upon this present hypothesis, that the sun and stars have no immaterial being residing in them, but are mere matter consisting of the subtlest particles and most vehemently agitated.

> For then we cannot but be assured that there is nothing in them more divine than what is seen in other things that shine in the dark suppose rotten wood, glo-worms or the flame of a rush-candle. (1656, 110)

We can see from the movement of More's argument that his position in the field of philosophy was precarious indeed. Caught between a vision of a world without spirit and that of a world that is nothing but spirit (and this before the emergence of Spinozism), More can do little more than pit these doctrines against each other. There is no middle ground; it is, rather, by his constant shifting from one side to the other, evoking spiritualism against materialism in another, that he hopes to open a space for true religion, the theoretical precariousness of which is thus revealed.

Yet, the encounter between occultism, puritan enthusiasm and materialism produces still another set of effects. The definition of the *anima mundi* as "The spirit or breath or wind of the world" reduces spirit to matter in the manner of Hobbes, suggesting that what we once considered immaterial and incorporeal really consists of subtle matter or subtle bodies. But the reduction of spirit does not stop here. The equivocity of the term "wind", its capacity to signify flatulence, permits not simply a reduction of spirit to subtle matter but to excrement, which thus comes to signify matter from which every trace of spirit has been extracted. Thus Swift's "excremental vision" is less a timeless account of the sublimation of a biologically given anal eroticism, "a discovery of the necessary relation between the higher and the lower" (Brown 1954) as the condition of culture *tout court*, than a historically quite specific effect of the disposition and hierarchical arrangement of philosophical doctrines. The disappearance of spirit from the world has not left behind a void; or, if it has, the void is immediately filled (Swift's nature like Aristotle's abhors a vacuum) with wind, vapors, effluvium and flatulence. The absent spirit has left in its wake a putrefying world whose atmosphere is thick with the stench of overripe matter. The world without spirit is nothing more than ordure: those who study it merely dabble in excrement. Here the text concentrates its force against materialism by evoking overwhelming disgust. We may recall Swift's portrait of the materialist philosopher in the "Digression Concerning Madness". In his "kennel" the philosopher appears as a

> surly, gloomy, nasty, slovenly mortal, raking in his own dung and dabbling in his urine. The best part of his diet is the reversion of his own

ordure which expiring into streams, whirls perpetually about and at last reinfunds. His complexion is of a dirty yellow, with a thin scattered beard exactly agreable to that of his dyet upon its first Declination; like other insects who having their birth and education in an excrement, from thence borrow their color and smell. (1958, 178)

The excremental imagery deployed against Swift's materialist adversaries is turned equally against religion itself: the excremental vision is truly a vision of the world, a way of imagining or figuring rather than conceptualizing matter without spirit. The disgust produced by the image of rot and excrement is symptomatic of a fantasy held in abeyance but not abandoned, that bodies contain souls, that the created world expresses the essence of its immaterial creator whose intention it fulfills. The merely material world is a degradation; we look inside man only to recoil in revulsion. It is a way of belittling and degrading what the text cannot help but pose as real; the material account of the madness of materialist philosophy, occultism and religion enthusiasm is disavowed in the same movement that puts it into play. The disgust that *A Tale* exhibits at certain points is thus a disgust at itself or at what it has itself constructed as the reality of human institutions and beliefs, as it refigures true religion with the false, ridiculing not simply Puritan doctrine but passages from the Holy Scripture itself. The very force of Swift's satire here carries it beyond itself, beyond its own limits. Section IX, in particular, shows the effect, inscribed in the letter of the text, of a satiric strategy that deprives itself of its own norms, in order to work more effectively. Dispersed and dissociated, the effects of the text's internal development are other than and opposed to the intention they were designed to serve. Thus, in the material/excremental world of which *A Tale* is a figuration, the idea of inspiration takes on a new meaning:

> At other times, were to be seen several hundreds linked together in a circular chain, with every many a part of belows applied to his neighbors breech, by which they blew up each other to the shape and size of a tun; and for that reason, with great propriety of speech did usually call their bodies, their vessels. When by these and the like performances, they were grown sufficiently replete they would immediately depart and disembogue for the public good, a plentiful share of their acquirements into their disciples chaps. (153)

As we have noted, the use of the materialist reduction of the non-corporeal to the corporeal against the Dissenters, ridiculing their religious acts as mere bodily functions, emphasizing the physicality of enthusiasm, can only turn against religion itself given the absence from the satire of any norm of true religion. If there is a norm or positive rule immanent in Swift's satire, it is like Spinoza's God, a cause that has disappeared into its effects, which in turn it cannot truly be said to have preceded. In fact, the movement of the *Tale*'s satire is the movement by which it divests itself of its founding intention (which is finally shown to have never been more than an external cover).

A Tale, however, does not simply reduce the world to matter and matter to excrement. While it is true that the work constructs a materiality (conceived negatively as the absence of spirit) to which it reacts with horror and disgust, this construction in no way entails a reduction of the complexity of the world and the plurality of its forms and modes. Instead, *A Tale* initiates a re-thinking of this complexity without reference to the opposition of matter and spirit. The absence of spirit may give rise to a sense of the world as excrement, but it does not prevent the positing of a plurality of materialities proper to it. The materiality of religion, for example, is a compound of corporeal (natural) and institutional (artificial) materialities. Our consideration of Aeolism raises the question that *A Tale* ceaselessly addresses without knowing it, not only in the unfolding of its narrative but even in the additions to its successive editions: what is the specific materiality of language?

"Books", wrote Sir William Temple, "are but dead instructors; which like a hand with an inscription, can point out the straight way upon the road, but can neither tell you the next turning, resolve you doubts or answer your questions" (1909, 26). Plato's critique of writing (*graphē*) opposes the natural, living, immaterial voice filled with the intelligence of the speaker to the artificial and merely material (*graphic*) nature of writing whose silence, density and opacity prevent it from bearing the intelligence in which it originates. In the *Phaedrus*, Socrates declares

> that writing has this strange quality and is very like painting; for the creatures of painting stand like living beings, but if one asks them a question, they preserve a solemn silence. And so it is with written words; you might think they spoke as if they had intelligence, but if you question them, wishing to know about their sayings, they always say one and the same thing. And every word when once it is written, is bandied about, both among those who understand and those who have no interest in it and it knows not to whom to speak or not to

speak; when ill-treated or unjustly reviled, it always needs its father to help it, for it has no power to protect itself. (Plato 1961, 521)

We have seen that Spinoza's *Tractatus Theologico-Politicus* sought for the first time to consider not what lay behind the Holy Scripture, animating it, filling its gaps, resolving its contradictions and conflicts, but rather the texture of the scripture itself as a linguistic artifact. Spinoza measured its joints and seams in order rationally to comprehend its specific compositeness, recording its contradictions and treating them as indispensable indices of the Bible's history. The prototype of all writing, of all scripture, that which once seemed to guarantee the presence of the animating, original intention in the material vehicle to which it had been entrusted, the Bible became a sinister confirmation of Plato's fears about writing: its mysteries were no longer signs of an infinite spiritual depth under the textual surface, of the reason that bound together its seemingly disparate parts, of the living voice that could be discerned even where the scripture seemed silent. In fact, in the light of Spinoza, what had once appeared to be mysteries were rather (philological or historical) problems and, as such, susceptible to a rational explanation based on a thorough knowledge of the languages in which the Scripture had originally been composed and of the history of those who had composed it. If the words of the Bible, the sounds or written marks, no longer effaced themselves before the intelligence that had produced them but instead formed dense, resistant, opaque and silent configurations on the surface of a text that had no depth, what might be said of lesser, merely human works?

In 1710, the fifth edition of *A Tale* appeared. The text differed substantially from the four previous editions: not only did it contain five prefatory and apologetic additions not to be found in the original text; it was also copiously annotated, the notes furnishing interpretive and exegetical aids (many of which were taken from Wotton's *Observations*). The text itself justified its own expansion. While "a great majority among the men of taste" approved of *A Tale*, "yet there have been two or three treatises written expressly against it, besides many others that have flirted at it occasionally, without one syllable having been ever published in its defense or even one quotation to its advantage, that I can remember except by the politic author of a late discourse between a Deist and a Socinian" (1958, 3). Given that "men of taste" comprised a tiny minority of the reading public, we may infer that *A Tale* has been generally misunderstood and misread. Thus what might have remained a biographical detail, a psychological rather than literary fact, is inscribed in the text itself. The additions serve two purposes: they are both defensive and interpretive. The term "apology" captures the inescapable equivocity of the new material, which simultaneously denies the validity of the criticisms levelled against the *Tale* and supplies what was obviously absent from the original text, namely, its true meaning and purpose as a satire against "the numerous and gross corruptions in Religion and Learning". In a fundamental way, Swift's disappointment with the reception of his work becomes *A Tale*'s confrontation with itself, with the actual effects that it has produced. It interiorizes hostile interpretations, hoping to turn them against themselves, as it has been turned against itself by its critics (and even its admirers). The fifth edition of *A Tale* marks the fact that Swift's intention had disappeared, like Spinoza's God, into the work of creation, intermingling and becoming confused with it, no longer separate from or prior to creation but identical to it and therefore subject to the laws that govern it.

In a certain sense, then, we can say that *A Tale* confronts its own materiality, that is, both its irreducibility to its founding intention and the fact that at the moment of its production it enters a network of causes and effects and as such is subject to forces far beyond the control or even the comprehension of the author. Wotton notes the fatal discrepancy between the intention that is stated at the outset of the work and its actuality, a discrepancy that traverses the text itself and that determines the effect that it will produce in a given historical situation. In Swift's attack on Rome and the Dissenters through Peter and Jack, Wotton declares "there might possibly be little harm" if not for

> the difference between the sharp and virulent books written in this age against any sect of Christians and those which were written about the beginning of the Reformation between the several contending parties then in Europe. For though the rage and spite with which men treated one another was as keen and as piquant then as it is now, yet the inclination of mankind was not then irreligious, and so their writings had little other effect but to increase men's hatred against any on particular sect, whilst Christianity, as such, was not nearly at all undermined. But now the common enemy appears bareface, and strikes in with some one or other sect of Christians, to wound the whole by that

means. And this is the case of this book, which is one of the profanest banters upon the religion of Jesus Christ, as such, that ever yet appeared. (1705, 324–5)

The conflict of forces (in this case, the partisans of spirit and the partisans of matter) that governs history has imposed a meaning on *A Tale*, irrespective of the intention that impelled it into existence. Such an imposition of meaning, however, is only made possible because the text possesses the very properties of which Plato (and Temple) spoke in his condemnation of writing. Only the density, opacity and paradoxically the brute silence of *A Tale* permits history thus to engrave its own meanings upon the surface of the text. The fifth edition of *A Tale* marks a kind of redoubling of the work upon itself, an attempt to efface itself (or rather to efface the properties, the possession of which renders it susceptible to history's interpretation and meanings). However, insofar as this double movement, this intervention, is itself an exercise of speech or writing, it simply reproduces the problem in a new form by giving rise to a new text that is itself a material artifact whose meaning is not governed by the author's intention but rather by a broader conflict of forces. Thus each apology, each explanation, requires further apology or explanation as the work regresses infinitely towards an undiscoverable intention, an immaterial sense lost amid bales of paper.

It is not surprising, then, that the year 1710 also marked the beginning of a sustained inquiry into the nature of language in general on Swift's part (*Prose Works* Vol. 4, xi–xv). In May 1712 this inquiry bore fruit: "A Proposal for Correcting, Improving and Ascertaining the English Tongue; in a letter to the most Honorable Robert, Earl of Oxford and Mortimer, Lord High Treasurer of Britain" (*Prose Works* Vol. 4, 1–21). This curious piece was dismissed by contemporaries as thinly disguised Tory propaganda (given the inordinately long tribute to Harley, one of the major leaders of the Tory Party), and by Samuel Johnson as having been written "without much knowledge of the general nature of language and without any accurate inquiry into the history of other tongues" (1905, Vol. 3, 16). If we take *A Tale* and the "Proposal" together, we may see the manner in which a certain conception of language or speech erupts within Swift's work, not as the result of a reasoned inquiry but rather as the element, internal yet foreign, finally unassimilable and unthinkable, within which Swift's work confronts its estrangement from itself, from what it was intended to be. Intention, meaning and truth disappear into the ineluctable materiality of the written word, which seems, as Plato feared, incapable of or unwilling to communicate its original truth, disseminating instead another truth, a second truth under whose solidity and density the first is buried. Accordingly, the very features of the "Proposal" that Johnson found so objectionable should not be taken simply as faults which would permit us to dismiss the text, but rather as symptoms which enjoin us to read it. For what is most curious about the essay is that it attempts (with great inconsistency) to deny the very qualities of language that Swift's work not only affirms but ceaselessly exploits (Wyrick 1988).

The proposal begins with the assertion "that our language is extremely imperfect; that its daily improvements are by no means in proportion to its daily corruptions; that the pretenders to polish and refine it, have chiefly multiplied abuses and absurdities; and that in many instances, it offends against every part of grammar" (*Prose Works*, Vol. 4, 6). To Swift, the English language has always lacked the refinement of Italian, Spanish and French for the simple reason that the roots of English are in Anglo-Saxon rather than Latin, and that Britain was never entirely subject to the domination of Rome (and presumably its civilizing influence). Even Latin, however, which is granted an unquestioned authority in Swift's text, suffered a rise and decline, testifying to one of the central anxieties of the "Proposal": unless certain measures are taken, the compositions of the present will be unintelligible and incomprehensible in a hundred years. This fear is born out not simply by the history of the English language to 1700 but also by the history of French and even Latin: "It is manifest that the Latin, three hundred years before Tully, was as unintelligible in his times, as the English and French of the same period are now" (8), The French of Swift's time "hath seen polishing as much as it will bear and appears to be declining", while "the English tongue is not arrived to such a degree of perfection as, upon that account, to make us apprehend any thoughts of its decay" (8). In a certain sense, change in language must also be decay insofar as change disrupts the identity of a language to itself, and sets it against itself so that its own past becomes unintelligible. It is precisely in this way that decline in language accompanies political decline. The past is no longer legible; it is immured in words and sentences that are irrevocably foreign. Its lessons, its wisdom, are hidden behind the opaque surface of a language that simultaneously is and is not ours.

Before the drift of language, however, Swift is not at all passive. If English could be "refined to a certain standard, perhaps there might be ways to fix it forever, or at least till we are invaded and made a conquest by some other state: and even then, our best writings might probably be preserved with care and grow into esteem and the authors have a chance for immortality" (8–9). To fix language forever, to render it once and for all identical and transparent to itself, its meanings forever present, this is the position to which the essay seeks to win its audience. We can see the theoretical fantasy underlying the "Proposal". The historicity of language is its downfall. For in the differentiations and mutations that constitute the history of language, language turns against itself, concealing in its novelty truths and meanings that it once manifested. To fix language is thus to deny its historicity by restoring language to what it perhaps once was and ideally ought to be: an instrument of communication, the fortunes of which depend upon the world that both communicates and is communicated. Swift seeks to restrict language to the functions of a medium that does not affect the meanings that it contains. It is no accident that Swift began work on the "Proposal" in the same year that he attempted to rectify the fatal discrepancy between the intended meaning of *A Tale* and the actual effects that it produced. The task was now to prevent language from obscuring or even concealing the meaning that it carries by somehow containing or controlling the one property that was as inescapable as it was troublesome: the stubborn materiality of language, its refusal to revert to an ideal, spiritual substance which would be beyond the corruption of matter.

But to fix a language forever means, equally, to reject the language as it is, or at least to reject its corruptions, affectations and useless conceits, and to restore it to its native purity. Accordingly, the high point of the development of English is said "to commence with the beginning of Queen Elizabeth's reign and to conclude with the great rebellion in forty-two" (9). The interregnum brought an excessive "infusion of enthusiastic jargon", while with the Restoration came the affectation typical of Charles II's court. Because they are external to the English language in its native state, the developments in language of the period following 1642 can be defined as excesses that hinder rather than help communication; they are, rather, signs of themselves than of the meanings they are designed to convey and as such they render language unintelligible to itself.

But even language restored to its purest state contains within itself, or in the elements and the sounds of which it is composed, a conflict between the material and the ideal or spiritual. It is not simply the link to antiquity that renders Latin, and languages derived from Latin, generally superior to English and the Germanic languages. Poets since the Restoration

> have introduced that barbarous custom of abbreviating words, to fit them to the measure of their verses; and this they have frequently done, so very injudiciously, as to form such harsh unharmonious sounds, that none but a *Northern* ear could endure. They have joined the most obdurate consonants without one intervening vowel only to shorten a syllable: and their taste in time became so depraved, that what was at first a poetical license not to be justified, they made their choice; alleging that the words pronounced at length, sounded faint and languid. (11)

Consonants, without the intervention of vowels, placed in abrupt propinquity, produce "so jarring a sound" that words and sentences become literally unutterable. The opposition of consonants and vowels, as conceived by Swift, reproduces the opposition to which it is irrevocably linked, the opposition of matter and spirit. For consonants (and *par excellence* the consonants typical of Northern European languages) are perpetual reminders of the very materiality of language that Swift constantly both affirms and denies. The "jarring" sounds and "roughness" of a language that is overflowing with untempered consonants and "overstocked with monosyllables" can only force a collapse of sense into sound, of intelligence into its material conveyance.

Further, the accumulation of consonants at the expense of vowels is the expression of a tendency peculiar to the northern nations to regress into barbarism: "this, perpetual disposition to shorten our words by retrenching the vowels, is nothing else but a tendency to lapse into the barbarity of those Northern Nations from whom we are descended and whose languages labour all under the same defect.... It is the same thing with respect to the politer arts among us; and the same defect of Heat which gives a fierceness to our nations, may contribute to the roughness of our language" (12). The proliferation of consonants and the decomposition of English into an accumulation of monosyllables is thus an eruption of brute nature, a "fierceness" of a nature that, in this case, far from being the source of order (Aristotle), dissociates, divides and renders meaningless. And if the nature to which the English language threatened perpetually to regress is decidedly Hobbesian, so are the means by which this regression may be forestalled, if not reversed. An institution like the *Academie Française* is needed to devise rules of usage and to enforce them. Above all, the purpose of such an institution would be the "ascertaining and fixing our language for ever, after such alterations are made in it as shall be thought requisite ... it is better a language should not be wholly perfect than that it should be perpetually changing and must give over at one time or other, or at length infallibly change for the worse" (14).

Although the stated aim of the proposed institution is to "fix language forever", the "Proposal" is clearly concerned less to prevent the addition of superfluous or harmful words and phrases than to *preserve* the language. As long as "no word, which a society shall give sanction to, be afterwards antiquated and exploded", the society Swift has in mind would "have liberty to receive whatever new ones they shall find occasion for: because then the old Books will yet be always valuable according to their intrinsic worth, and not thrown aside on account of unintelligible words and phrases which appear harsh and uncouth, only because they are out of fashion" (15). A dehiscence thus sets the origin of language against its natural destiny; the English language will only be extricated from its natural fierceness and harshness through the efforts of an institution capable of taming it. Left to itself, without the intervention of human institutions, the English language, already separated by history from the wisdom of antiquity, threatens in its very development "to lapse into the barbarity of those Northern nations from whom we are descended and whose languages all labour under the same defect" (12). The "Grand Academy" that Swift projects would render language forever intelligible to itself by suspending its immanent development, its own tendency to dissociate from itself. Further, such an institution would act to check the native disposition of English to eliminate its vowels while producing an overabundance of harsh and jarring consonants. In short, a British Academy would protect the English language from its own peculiar materiality, its tendency to revert to its material elements.

Even the first edition of *A Tale* – *A Tale* before it confronted the problem of its reception – posited a similar relation between the material properties of language and the problem of enduring intelligibility. Thus the "Dedication to Prince Posterity" exhibits more than simply a desire for literary immortality and a corresponding fear of mutability. In a note added in 1710, Swift explains that "it is the usual style of decried writers to appeal to posterity, who is here represented as a prince in his nonage and time as his governor and the author begins in a way very frequent with him, by personating other writers who sometimes offer such reasons and excuses for publishing their works don't deserve to be preserved by prosperity" (30). As usual, however, the laments of the narrator about the destiny of his writing are not clearly and consistently differentiated from the anxieties about language and writing that recur throughout *A Tale*. The "personation" fades before the very images it raises. The speaker conjures up the "vast flourishing body" of modern authors and we see the fear of the mob, the mass, that appears so frequently in *A Tale*. As the introduction informs us, "whoever hath an ambition to be heard in a crowd, must press and squeeze and thrust and climb with indefatigable pains ... it being as hard to get quit of number as of hell" (55). But the proliferation of authors characteristic of the modern age, a process linked to the blurring of social stations, does not lead to a corresponding propagation of learning or a more extensive and therefore democratic dissemination of truth. On the contrary, the sheer number of texts obscures the distinctions between individual words, and quality reverts to mere quantity. Prince posterity will never see even the "first-rate" poets who themselves number 136, each possessed of "large comely volumes ready to show for a support to his pretensions" (33). Learning necessarily declines in proportion as the number of writings increases, every text competing with every other text, with all finally obscured as texts, visible only as paper and ink.

> When I first thought of this address, I had prepared a copious list of titles to present your highness as an undisputed argument for what I affirm. The originals were posted fresh upon all gates and corners of streets; but returning in a very few hours to take a review, they were all torn down and fresh ones in their places. I inquired after them among readers and booksellers, but I inquired in vain; the memorial of them was lost among men; their place was no more to be found. (34–5)

Language folds back upon itself in its materiality to bury the truth or meaning which it is supposed to reveal. While the Dedication undoubtedly contains a satiric attack against those whose writings deserve to perish, it exhibits alongside this satire a fear that the text it introduces will be buried under a mountain of paper. Its truth will be lost among men, given that it will be indistinguishable from the mob of texts above which it seeks (but how successfully?) to climb. The text becomes a material object among others, no longer the envelope of incorporeal truth but, rather, in its very substantiality the corpse of meaning and intention, mere body from which spirit has departed. Swift is thus left with a paradox: the very materiality of writing, that which allows it to exist separately and beyond its author (for posterity) subverts the intention that impelled it into existence.

The "Proposal", like *A Tale*, exhibits a singular fascination with the corporeality of language, its physical properties. But the corporeality of language is not the same as its materiality. The former is rather a sign of the latter, a way of conceptualizing the inconceivable or of figuring the unimaginable and the unthinkable. We have seen that even Plato, in his discussion of what we have called the materiality of language, employed physical metaphors to capture a sense of the irreducibility of the written word to its original intention, stressing first its "graphic" character and then its silence and deadness. We ought to keep this fact in mind when we read a passage such as the following from the introduction to *A Tale*:

> air being a heavy body and therefore (according to the system of Epicurus) continually descending must needs to be more so, when loaden and pressed down by words; which are also bodies of much weight and gravity, as it is manifest from those deep impressions they make and leave upon us; and therefore must be delivered from a due altitude or else they will neither carry a good aim nor fall down with a sufficient force. (60)

Few twentieth-century commentaries on *A Tale* have failed to note the obvious play on the ambiguities of "weight", "gravity" and "impressions" which exploits the separation of literal (or physical) from the metaphorical by reducing the latter to the former. This passage is usually said to ridicule the failure of modern thinking to distinguish between the literal and metaphorical senses of words such as "spirit" (to take an example from the previous chapter).

Yet we have seen from the example of Hobbes that such reductions of the metaphorical to the literal, of the spiritual to the material, were not simply errors of reasoning (nor was Swift naive enough to regard them as such). Instead, they were generally effective tactical devices designed to alter the relation of forces between spirit and matter in the conceptual domain, to evict incorporeal and immaterial causes from certain designated fields. Swift may render temporarily laughable Hobbes's mechanistic physiology, and twentieth-century critics may join in the laughter from the vantage point of post-mechanistic physiologies, but neither the historical importance of mechanistic physiology or of Hobbes's uncompromising exclusion of spirit from his unbounded universe will thus be altered (Gargani 1971). Seen in relation to Swift's concern with language in general and with the unforeseen and apparently uncontrollable reception of his own works in particular, the above passage from the introduction to *A Tale* does not exhaust itself in the operation of satire, but is instead caught up in a network of discourses and conflicts external to *A Tale* and made to return against itself.

The wordplay upon which the humor of the passage depends (the play on "might", "gravity" and "impressions") alludes, insofar as it touches on the question of language, to the very anxieties that traverse Swift's *oeuvre*. In according a figuration of the corporeality of language, Swift invokes the notion of its materiality. For only by granting a certain physicality to language can the mode of being proper to it, and even more the peculiar force that language possesses, be designated. At one point, insinuated into the Introduction immediately following the play on the weight and gravity of words and the "deep impressions they leave upon us", is a passage from Lucretius's *De Rerum Natura*. The two lines from Lucretius (and this may be said to be true of Swift's use of Epicurus and Lucretius in general) displace the equivocity that permits the play in the preceding lines. The distinction between the literal and the metaphorical (and by implication between the material and the spiritual) is transformed into a distinction between modalities of matter.

Lucretius writes: *Corporean quoque enim vocem constare fatendum est. Et Sonitum, quoiniam possunt impelleve Sensus.* In a footnote, Swift supplies Thomas Creech's translation (1683): "Tis Certain then, that Voice that thus can wound Is all Material; Body every Sound" (1958, 60). The section of Book IV of *De Rerum Natura* from which the passage has been extracted deals with the problem of audition, that is, the problem of how "sound and voice" (*sonus et vox*) become audible and intelligible, how they produce the effects that they are observed to produce. We can see that this problem has a curious relation to the set of problems that we have designated as central to Swift's work at least through 1712. For Lucretius (and by extension for Epicurus) all that is capable of producing an effect must be composed of body. Sounds and voices, because they evoke responses, must be corporeal. In order to demonstrate that voice and sound are corporeal, and further, to deduce the particular corporeality proper to them, Lucretius examines the effects of sound and voice on senses other than hearing. He notes in particular that "*praeterea radit vox fauces saepe facitque asperiora foras gradiens arteria clamor*" ("Besides, the voice often scrapes the throat and a shout roughens the windpipe on its outward path") (Lucretius 1975, Vol. 4, 525–8). The roughness that for Lucretius proves that language is composed of bodies is the very roughness that Swift finds disagreeable in the English language and that he seeks to control, if not eliminate. The very property that allows language to function, its corporeality, is thus for Swift neither simply an absurdity of Epicurean philosophy to be laughed at, nor a literal, physical truth in search of its metaphorical, spiritual complement. Rather, it is a metonym that represents the irreducible materiality of language.

We have seen that the authority of a judge or a Bishop arises not from natural and essential causes but from causes as artificial and external as their clothes; that law and religion are not spiritual but material truths. In a similar way, the specific materiality of language appears inseparable from its various institutional settings. The Introduction to *A Tale* offers a number of cases in which a series of commonplace metonyms are inverted. The pulpit in its limited (literal and material) sense can function metonymically to designate the whole of religion. *A Tale* instead collapses the whole into the part. The pulpit has no sense beyond its existence as an "edifice", a "machine". The different types of pulpit are to be distinguished only by the sort of timber from which they have been fabricated. Again, the satire on Hobbesian materialism is obvious. The playful abuse of metaphor is certainly designed to ridicule materialist reduction. But this particular instance of "literalization" is no less complex than the other examples we have examined.

Speech has no meaning in and of itself. Its peculiar force derives from the materiality of its setting. The case of the Church is particularly instructive. As Swift argues in the *Letter concerning the Test* and the *Argument Against Abolishing Christianity*, a prayer uttered in the physical confines of an Anglican church and accompanied by the bodily actions prescribed by Church doctrine possesses a different meaning than the same prayer uttered outside that setting. Even in the absence of belief, even given an intention at odds with the conventional meaning of the prayer, the sounds emitted by the vocal chords together with the appropriate bodily actions are sufficient. Opposing words uttered in the heart are eclipsed, if not effaced, by an overwhelming institutional materiality, the complexity of which is condensed into the single phrase "mandatory conformity" (even if only occasional). The most seditious thoughts of the most fanatic Dissenter are rendered "immaterial" in both senses of the word by his merely corporeal participation in a Church thus reduced to a materiality no less brutal than that of Swift's pulpit. We ought to remember that the doctrine of forcing by threat of punishment either the Dissenter or the unbeliever into physical conformity to doctrines he did not accept was widely regarded by moderate churchmen as hypocritical and by those outside the established church as a sign of the absolutist pretensions of the High Church faction. A precise combination of vowels and consonants is thus not infused with the spirit, understanding and sentiment of the speaker's mind, from which on the contrary it appears to be independent. Instead, their meaning is determined from without, by a certain posture of the body, the space in which the body is placed, and the disposition of forces that determined the body to be in that place.

The corporeality of speech is of course denounced in *A Tale* (and not merely parodied), only to re-emerge in the denunciation itself as the dregs, the excrement of which language cannot seem to rid itself. At the most primary level, the materiality of speech is linked to the possibility of a text yielding meanings other than those intended by the author. One of the central themes in the satire on Catholicism is the abuse of Scripture. Interpretive methods more closely resemble strategies designed to force a text into yielding meanings opposed to those it seeks to convey. But the question that seems always to haunt *A Tale* is how are such abuses possible? What property or properties permit utterances to mean something other than what they were intended to mean by the understanding in which they originated?

Following Swift's allegory, the three brothers want to alter the coat their father left in accordance with fashion. The father, however, left a will providing "full instructions in every particular concerning the wearing and management" of the coats (1958, 84). The will does not provide for the alteration in question, namely the addition of shoulder knots to the coats. Peter, the most learned of the brothers, then puts to work an interpretive apparatus that functions by reducing words to their constituent elements: first syllables, and then letters themselves. Thus he is able to find S, H, O, U, L, D, E, R. Only the letter K remains lacking. Peter then resorts to the historical argument that "K was a illegitimate modern letter, unknown to learned ages nor anywhere to be found in ancient manuscripts" (84). Thus C is replaced by K and "KNOT" is arrived at.

Interpretation thus overturns the domination of spirit over letter and, like modern criticism, as it is depicted in section III of *A Tale*, substitutes "superficies" for significance and "excrescence" for what is intrinsic. The ancient critics, a race "for some ages utterly extinct", performed exactly the opposite operation. They know that true reading consists of dividing "every beauty of matter or of struggle from the corruption that apes it". Even this species of critic seemingly set up as a prescription for the activity proper to the critic, must in the course of reading exercise "The caution of a man that walks through Edinburgh streets in a morning who is indeed as careful as he can to watch diligently and spy out the filth in his way; not that he is curious to observe the colour and complexion of the ordure, or take its dimensions, much less to be paddling in, or tasting it; but only with a design to come out as clearly as he may" (84). Textual excrescences become excrement. What is irreducible in the text to its founding intention refuses simply to disappear. At its most benign, textual materiality appears as the "luxuriant, the rotten, the dead, the sapless and the overgrown branches" of works which the critics like Pausanias' ass can nibble on. At the other extreme, however, the critic's enlightened gaze only causes the ordure or textual excrement to fester more fulsomely. Thus Swift links the irreducibility of letter to spirit to that of bodies to souls with the disgust symptomatic of his peculiar excremental materialism.

4

Gulliver's Travels:
Quarrels with Nature

We have seen that *A Tale* finally doubles back upon itself in a futile attempt to add to the letter of the work the spirit that has vanished into it, but that the spirit of the addition itself disappears into the corporeality of writing. What appears as an attempt to mediate between the spirit behind or prior to the work and its material existence succeeds only in extending its very materiality. It is in this sense that, as the prefatory pieces tell us, the original manuscript has been lost. The manuscript from which the actual book was produced is a mere copy (and a defective one at that) and the author was not present to oversee the publication. An absent author and the lost original: these are not fictions but truths designed to be taken as falsehoods. *Gulliver's Travels*, in contrast, exhibits no such concern to supply absent meanings or to mediate the contradictions engendered by the narrative. No interpretive gloss or explanatory notes are added to the text. While it is true that the prefatory "Letter from Captain Gulliver to his Cousin Sympson" which first appeared in the version of *Gulliver's Travels* in the Faulkner edition of Swift's works in 1735, asserts that the "original manuscript is all destroyed" (*Prose Works*, Vol. 11, 7), Swift appears (with this brief disclaimer issued by Gulliver who is consistently presented as the author of the *Travels*) content to let the work stand on its own.

But of course it does not stand on its own and never has. From the moment of its appearance an immense interpretive apparatus, which has not to this day ceased to proliferate, has grown up around *Gulliver's Travels*. In the months immediately following its publication at the end of October 1726, the first two books, the voyages to Lilliput and Brobdingnag, became the objects of an unusual amount of commentary. Not only were interpretations of the "allegory" offered in numerous journals, but actual keys and glosses appeared, most of which attempted to establish correspondences between the characters and places that appear in the four voyages and the British political scene of the preceding century. After its meaning was thus established, the work was enrolled in the ranks of the opposition to Walpole's Whig regime.[1] But, apart from a few central figures, like the Lilliputian Treasurer Flimnap in whom most commentators have been able to discern a resemblance to Walpole, the allegorical method seems only to have led to a plurality of competing explanations, the adjudication of whose claims appears impossible.

Accordingly, the quest for univocal meaning has led to a gradual, but by no means complete, abandonment of the allegorical reading in favor of methods that appeared more likely to unify the text around a clearly identifiable intention. At the same time, the allegorical reading of of of *Gulliver's Travels*, with its insistence on connecting textual and historical particulars, ran afoul of the dominant trends in twentieth-century literary criticism, with their insistence on the ahistoricity and formal closure of literary works. If the tendency to allegorize has survived at all it is only insofar as it has been tempered by the demand that literary texts, at least those that are deemed superior, must not be too tied to historical particularity, but instead express universal and eternal concerns. So, for one recent critic, if it is true that *Gulliver's Travels* is an attack on the Whig state, the Whig state is itself only the particular (and by no means only possible) manifestation of the general evil that is properly the object of Swift's satire (Lock 1980, 2).

As might be expected, however, attention in our own time has tended to shift away from the historical problems and references of the first two voyages toward the seemingly more universal themes exhibited in the fourth voyage, the voyage to the Houyhnhnms. Even here the commentaries have failed to demonstrate the controlling intention or the object of the satire. The Houyhnhnms, the Yahoos, Gulliver as narrator, even the minor character Pedro de Mendez (the Portuguese sea captain who rescues Gulliver and returns him to Europe at the end of the voyages), all pose seemingly insurmountable problems for interpretation. As is well known, by the late 1960s, two opposing schools of interpretation emerged: the so-called hard and soft schools, the former stressing Swift's pessimism and the attack on the human per se, and the latter arguing that the satire is turned against Gulliver

himself and that his condemnation of European culture and institutions is to be discounted.[2] A much smaller number of critics
have noted the "disarray" of *Gulliver's Travels* as a whole, or of
certain individual books, occasionally identifying interesting discrepancies, only to subordinate explanation of the work to judgment which compares *Gulliver's Travels* to an ideal type and finds
it wanting (Quintana 1936; Carnochan 1968).

At the same time, there is no question of having merely to "set
aside" erroneous interpretations to allow the work spontaneously
to emanate its truth to us in the luminosity of its empirical existence. For the work itself says what it says, and it is not the task
of the critic to repeat that discourse but to produce the theory of
its conditions of possibility. To remove conceptual obstacles such
as the postulate of textual unity is to open the way, beyond either
a devaluation or an idealization of the work, to a theory capable
of rendering it intelligible in the complexity specific to it, and in
fact on the very basis of this complexity. For to read works as a
materialist is not to impose on or discern in them *a* contradiction
whose form and internal relations never vary, and which would
persist in an essential identity from work to work, changing only
in its content. On the contrary, it is to grasp through a "concrete
analysis of a concrete (textual) situation" the way in which each
text constitutes a singular realization of ideological struggle. As
we have seen from *A Tale of a Tub*, texts erect a multiplicity of
possible defenses against the specific truths that they produce but
cannot, must not, acknowledge – truths, the denial, undoing or
isolation of which constitutes the concrete development of the
work.

If, as we have argued, Swift wrote from within the ideological
apparatus of the Church of England, and if its conflicts are inescapably inscribed in the letter of his work, it is incumbent upon
us to show how this history is present in *Gulliver's Travels*, as an
objective determination that composes the work at the cost of
disordering it, setting it against itself even as it projects the form
that it can never finally achieve. In particular, how does *Gulliver's
Travels* bear the marks of the antagonisms generated by the political and philosophical crisis of Anglicanism? The concerns of
Gulliver's Travels are not those of *A Tale*, written twenty years earlier. It is not the constellation of conflicts surrounding the emergent materialisms of the seventeenth century that haunts *Gulliver's
Travels*, but the new way of imagining society and political order

that arose with but remained distinct from (and, in certain respects, even opposed to) these materialisms. We may refer to an apparatus of thought that, however divergent and even antagonistic the distinct theoretical practices of which it was composed, defined a problematic profoundly disturbing to the Anglican political doctrines that preceded it, a problematic whose diffusion through the political discourse of the time only underscored the discrepancy between the spontaneous political philosophy of the Anglican church and historical reality.

This problematic is of course that of nascent liberalism, which Pierre-François Moreau in his *Le récit utopique* has more accurately called "a juridical anthropology" (1981, 9). It emerged through the writings of Suarez, Grotius, Hobbes and Locke among others, although it does not, insofar as it can be said to comprise a unified field, coincide with any particular thinker or text. In certain cases (for example, Hobbes) the premisses of a body of philosophical work may be said to belong to this new problematic while his conclusions do not. In other cases (for example, Grotius), the inverse may be true. We can, however, describe the essential characteristics of this problematic, the problematic to which *Gulliver's Travels* constitutes a response, as it took shape across diverse political doctrines (absolutism and republicanism) and texts.

First, in counterposition to the Aristotelian–medieval view of the world as ordered according to God's providential design, the natural world (of which human beings were seen as part) was deprived of its end(s) and subject to a profound disordering, the image of which was most acutely provided by Hobbes's description of bodies propelled into endless motion without prior purpose or ultimate aim. Second, as a part of this natural state, humanity was itself disaggregated, no longer Aristotle's *zoon politikon* organically (as it would be said in later ages) and originally united in a community, but reduced to solitary individuals, the association of which became increasingly difficult to conceive and possessed of no other end but that of the gratification of seemingly incompatible appetites and lusts. Prior to their association, individuals trapped or free (depending on one's perspective) in what came to be called the state of nature were autonomous and, what is of capital importance, equal. Their equality was not simply a matter of their physical and intellectual powers, it was even more an original equality of right (although the former might serve as a foundation or proof of the latter). Third, to escape the state of

nature (which might be pictured as impossible or merely incon-
venient), human beings were said to have overcome their mutual
antagonism by creating an artificial civil state founded by a contract to which the individuals concerned voluntarily consented,
and thus transferred their original right to self-government to the
sovereign or the state. Fourth, whatever inequalities subsequently
arose in the civil or social state (inequalities of property, political
power and rank) to supplant the natural equality of all men were
therefore purely artificial and moreover were founded on the
consent of (at least a majority of) the individuals who comprise a
given society. Finally, individuals become more than subjects of
the authority of the state or monarch; they become subjects in the
modern sense, that is, originally equal legal actors or authors,
possessed of rights such that their servitude or subordination could
only (at least *de jure*) have been freely willed.[3]

The fact that Swift is sometimes identified with this tradition,
usually on the basis of his use of the notion of "consent" in his
arguments for the political independence of Anglo-Colonial
Ireland, makes an examination of *Gulliver's Travels*, written during
the period of his most intense involvement in Irish affairs, all the
more necessary. For just as *A Tale of a Tub* exhibits Swift's enduring attachment to the increasingly unthinkable philosophies incarnate in the institution of the Anglican Church, so does *Gulliver's
Travels* manifest not a set of arguments against but rather a refusal,
a denial, not only of the various doctrines of nascent liberalism
but, more fundamentally, of the problematic within which these
doctrines took shape. This denial or refusal is of course a defense:
a defense of doctrines no longer regarded as valid from within an
institution that is itself an island separated by great gulfs from the
world around; an island in time – in, but in an important sense
not of, early capitalist Britain.

Interpretations of *Gulliver's Travels* have tended to focus on the
effects of Swift's irony, on the meaning – ethical, philosophical
and political – of the discrepancies that so often appear between
Gulliver's descriptions and the meaning he attaches to them, or
his reports of conversations and his interpretation of them. While
Swift's irony remains of central importance and continues to merit
critical examination, the philosophico-political positions immanent
in *Gulliver's Travels* are also and perhaps more fundamentally displayed in ways that have ostensibly been overlooked because they
seem so obvious. But, read in the light of the problematic of

juridical anthropology, the obvious becomes as important as, if not more important than, the formal devices and the hidden meanings they appear to produce. Swift's response to this problematic is not to be found in the statements of characters whose views seem privileged in the text (the king of Brobdingnag, Lord Munodi and the Houyhnhnm master), nor even in the distance between the truths such characters utter and Gulliver's grasp of them. It is, rather, to be found in the narrative itself, in what happens, in the conditions that make possible the utterances of these privileged characters, not so much what is said (by Gulliver or by authoritative figures) as the nature, the "staging", of the voyages themselves in the most banal detail – "what the work is compelled to say in order to say what it wants to say" (Macherey 1978, 94).

Thus, despite the nearly total absence of philosophical references, *Gulliver's Travels* is a profoundly philosophical work, bearing within itself philosophical positions that it illustrates rather than states, that it exhibits but does not name or explain. But, to specify the doctrine or doctrines immanent in *Gulliver's Travels* is not to read the work as an expression of a philosophy all the while possessed of a unity that only escaped earlier readers because they did not know its secret, because while they could read what it said, they could not see what it showed. To say that *Gulliver's Travels* constitutes simultaneously a defense and a refusal is not to say that it succeeds in either of these projects, or that the positions immanent within it are not themselves traversed with contradictions. On the contrary, *Gulliver's Travels* is the putting to work, or putting into play, of certain theoretical positions in a way that not only exposes but even heightens and intensifies their internal contradictions.

Gulliver, unlike his predecessor, Robinson Crusoe, never returns to a state of nature, a point of origin in theory or in fact from which the solitary individual "discovers" other dissociated individuals and negotiates the social bond through the transfer of natural right. There is no state of nature in *Gulliver's Travels* and for good reason. Gulliver's travels do not lead him to empty spaces or desert islands. The world is a social plenitude, its spaces already full. There is no place outside of or prior to human society in which Gulliver is free (or forced) to invent or re-invent culture: society always already exists. As an individual, he must conform to already established practices and customs. But *Gulliver's Travels* does not simply reject by the movement of its narrative the state of nature as a historical fact; it rejects such a concept even as a theoretical possibility. The work constitutes a figuration of the natural and thus irreducible sociability that is proper to humankind, a sociability that, as it is assumes the form specific to *Gulliver's Travels*, produces a series of political effects which can be enumerated as a series.

Among the most obvious is that the book constitutes a rejection of the narrative of discovery: Gulliver discovers nothing; or, rather, he discovers Lilliput or Brobdingnag in the sense that one "discovers" Paris or London. There is no land to be discovered in the modern sense, that is, discovered to be destitute like Locke's "wild woods and uncultivated waste" (Locke 1980, 24), wanting only to be appropriated by a productive humanity. Neither are there lands populated only by human savages who, having failed to rise to the threshold of sociality, are condemned to live in a state of permanent war or at least insecurity; dissociated individuals or perhaps small families without law or morality or benefit of culture and to whom conquest alone can bring peace and prosperity (a conquest which, for Hobbes and Locke, can be seen as an effect of the consent, whether tacit or active, of the conquered). On the contrary, Gulliver encounters worlds that can only be described as civilized and whose laws, customs and letters are recorded with all the detail that Swift's parody of realist narratives requires, with the obvious result that the colonial enterprise, along with the philosophical arguments that support it, becomes indefensible, nothing more than another example of the malicious conduct that Gulliver comes to see as proper to mankind.

Hence, consider Swift's well-known attack on colonialism at the conclusion of the work. Nothing could be gained, he tells us, from the colonization of Lilliput, which is "hardly worth the charge of a fleet and army to reduce them" (*Prose Works* Vol. 11, 293). Of course, this argument based on "policy" or self-interest calls attention to another argument, deferred but never abandoned, marked by its very exclusion as primary: the argument based on justice. Beneath the irony there is the recognition that an English attack on Lilliput would be the equivalent of the Lilliputian scheme of "reducing the whole empire of Blefuscu to a province and governing it by a viceroy", and "of reducing a free and brave people to slavery" (53) that Gulliver so strenuously opposed. Continuing to argue from policy, that is, strategically, ostentatiously refraining from any appeal to justice, he suggests that both Brob-dingnag and the flying Island of Laputa are too formidable militarily for Europeans to attempt colonization. But the irony fades before the example of the Houyhnhnms: Gulliver refuses any proposal "for conquering that magnanimous nation" (237). Finally, the absence of any pre-social state of savagery and the appearance of an already socialized world lead to a denunciation of colonialism in general:

> But I had another reason which made me less forward to enlarge his majesty's dominions by my discoveries. To say the truth, I had con-ceived a few scruples with relation to the distributive justice of princes upon those occasions. For instance, a crew of pirates are driven by a storm they know not whither, at length a boy discovers land from the topmast, they go on shore to rob and plunder, they see an harmless people, are entertained with kindness, they give the country a new name, they take formal possession of it for the king, they set up a rotten plank or stone for a memorial, they murder two or three dozen of the natives, bring away a couple more by force for a sample, return home and get a pardon. Here commences a new dominion acquired with a title by *divine right*. Ships are sent with the first opportunity, the natives driven out or destroyed, their princes tortured to discover their gold, a free license given to all acts of inhumanity and lust, the earth reeking with the blood of its inhabitants: and this execrable crew of butchers employed in so pious an expedition, is a modern colony sent to convert and civilize an idolatrous and barbarous people. (294)

The object of the satire would appear to be the colonial prac-tices of the Spanish, especially those employed in the conquest of Mexico (which are also singled out for criticism in *Robinson Crusoe*), and the doctrine of divine right, which, although it employed the language of law ("dominion"), was in fact designed to justify the arbitrary and lawless use of force to enlarge the domain and there-fore the wealth of the reigning sovereign. A mainstay of anti-Catholic and anti-Spanish (and later anti-French) propaganda was the detailed depiction of the horrors of the destruction of the Aztec and Inca civilizations. Yet, far from leading to a revulsion towards colonialism in general, such propaganda encouraged the British public to differentiate between good and bad colonialism, between the lawful and lawless, just and unjust, conquest of other nations (better to enslave a people than to exterminate them, and better yet to make them mere servants rather than slaves). But Swift indulges in a rather conventional denunciation of the colonial

131

theory and practice of others only in order to lure the reader into occupying a position from which even "good" and "just" colonial practices and theories become vulnerable to Gulliver's scathing critique, which is at that very point abruptly subject to an ironic reversal:.

> But this description, I confess, doth by no means affect the British nation, who may be an example to the whole world for their wisdom, care and justice in planting colonies. (294)

In fact, Swift's attack on the apparently lawless practices of the *conquistadors* and their justification by appeal to the divine right of the sovereign in whose name they acted is a displacement: the doctrine of the divine right of Christian princes to oppose paganism and idolatry everywhere they encountered them, and to coerce infidels into practicing (if not believing) the true faith, occupied only a minor place in the hierarchy of justifications of European conquest and empire. Within a few decades of the conquest, the Spanish state itself showed a profound concern to establish a legality proper to colonialism (Hanke 1959; Pagden 1990, 1–13). Out of the debates and controversies that followed emerged the two great theoreticians of international law and of the rights of war in the sixteenth and early seventeenth centuries: Francisco Vitoria and Francisco Suarez. These philosophers took very seriously the rights of nations, as well as the rights of individuals, both of which were regarded as equal before the law: the idea that pagans, and by extension nations composed of pagans, possessed no rights was abominable to them. Vitoria and Suarez were interested in defining the rights proper to man as man, and nation as nation prior to religious beliefs and institutions (Moreau 1981, 132–4).

Such seemingly liberal concerns, however, in no way invalidated or even called into question the colonial enterprise, they only required that colonialism be theorized and legitimated in a different way. Thus Suarez, who rejected any essential political or juridical distinction between Christians and infidels, and by extension any notion of a natural hierarchy of races, did not seek to declare the enslavement of the Indians unjust, but only to provide it with a new foundation: the notion of the individual as owner (*dominus*) of his own freedom who had the right voluntarily to enslave himself to another (Tuck 1979, 56). "Because man is the owner of his freedom, he can sell or alienate it" (Suarez 1944, Vol. 2, 269).[4] Similarly, Vitoria rejected the right of Christian states to make war on the infidels in order to convert them. But if the infidels refused to allow Catholic priests to preach the gospel among them (285) or to grant Spanish armies safe passage through their dominions (278–84) (a right, it should be noted, that few European states granted their neighbors), then war against them was justified under international law (even if, Vitoria adds, it is not always prudent to engage in war) (285).

Thus Spanish colonialism was in no way characterized by arbitrary policies, by a flagrant disregard for law and the rights of individuals and nations. On the contrary, it is hardly an exaggeration to say that it gave rise to modern international law; and Spanish policy was constantly adjusted to conform to a strict legality. The rise of a juridical ideology scrupulously concerned with the rights of individuals and nations in no way impeded or even made more human the rise of colonialism. During Swift's lifetime, when the center of colonial initiative had shifted from the Iberian peninsula to France and England, the distance between liberal philosophy, with its guarantees and promises, and the actual conditions of the individuals and nations who were supposed to benefit from the conscientious observation of legality had perhaps never been greater. The violence inflicted on millions of people in the Americas and in Africa was precisely not illegal or arbitrary; on the contrary, it was regulated by a legal system (or systems) that surpassed even the canon of Roman law in its comprehensiveness and coherence.[5] At the very moment the English had formulated their Declaration of Rights in the face of the threat of absolutism, they were occupied in acquiring a monopoly in the slave trade to the Americas (John Locke himself was a shareholder in the Royal African Company) and in making war against the Indians who lived in proximity to English colonies. But again, as philosophers and politicians were careful to show, these actions, despite appearances, were carried out with the strictest concern for justice. It took a philosopher of Locke's abilities to show that the land that the Indians and their ancestors had occupied for a millennium could not rightfully be claimed by them as their property (according to the criteria presented in the fifth chapter of the *Second Treatise of Government*) and was thus available to the Europeans to appropriate in all justice; and that, further, if the Indians resisted the European appropriation and development of these common lands, it is they who would be guilty of injustice and thereby liable to punishment by states or individuals. In the same way, while Locke's denunciations of slavery are well known, the slavery with which he was most concerned was that of property owners who suffered under a despotic regime in whose eyes the property rights of individuals were not absolute. The enslavement of Africans, in contrast, could be justified (as indeed it was by the Royal African Company) on the condition that they were prisoners taken in combat in a just war (Davis 1966, 183):

> the power a conqueror gets over those he overcomes in a just war is perfectly despotical: he has an absolute power over the lives of those, who, by putting themselves in a state of war, have forfeited them. (Locke 1980, 93)

It was thus not a matter of hypocrisy that the Europeans spoke of rights even as they violated them, but that the discourse of juridical anthropology was itself a weapon (and an important one) in the arsenal of colonialism, justifying in the most cunning ways any conquest of lands and peoples that the disparity between powers would permit. Like the Lilliputian emperor's declarations of leniency, the discourses of inalienable rights and freedoms, and of the purely voluntary subjection of individuals and nations, were brought like the plague to those who lacked sufficient force to deter or repel their would-be liberators, the bearers of civilization, and the rule of law. No greater misfortune could befall the inhabitants of Africa and the Americas than to be declared by the Europeans to live in a pre-social state of nature: the lands that they inhabited were sure to be taken, as armies and navies arrived to assist their voluntary subjection to a legal state whose institutions would ensure their transition to a civilized condition. In *Gulliver's Travels* it is not merely lawless power and arbitrary rule – the abnormal condition that disrupts the ordinary course of a legality whose order is obvious to anyone – but even more legal violence, the horror that is precisely not exceptional but regular, internal to law's empire, the rapine that it both incites and justifies, that becomes visible. In the light of the historical reality of colonialism, Swift's remark that British colonies, as opposed to the lawless variety typical of absolutist states, are administered with "strict regard to the distribution of justice" is doubly ironic. It is not simply that the British in fact have no regard for the distribution of justice; it is perhaps even more importantly that the justice they distribute is itself an instrument of injustice according to Swift's norms. Whatever his intentions and despite his own participation in an institution of a colonial outpost, Swift, insofar as he rejects the juridical ideology of early modern Europe, is led to (state) a rejection of the colonial enterprise in even its most modern form. The supreme irony is that Swift's arguments (both rational and rhetorical) for the independence of the colony from the metropole would, by the end of the eighteenth century, be appropriated by the Catholic masses in their struggle to free themselves from Protestant domination, an important component of which remained the Anglican Church. Once again, Swift's most successful writing only served his enemies and undermined the foundations of the institutions he sought to defend.

Although *Gulliver's Travels* is not a narrative of discovery, it is not quite true that Gulliver discovers no uninhabited space, no desert island. At the beginning of his third voyage, after being set adrift by pirates, he makes his way to a small group of unpopulated islands. Even the largest of them, however, is nothing more than a great rock which, although it appears to afford the barest necessities of food and water, offers no real possibilities, no potential, for a solitary but productive life. Swift thus offers a paradoxical figuration of what Hobbes and Locke refer to as the state of nature. Locke's state of nature is bountiful (at least once it is "mixed" with human labor) and spacious, and life there is for the most part orderly and tolerable. Hobbes's state of nature, however bleak it is (and it is far less tolerable than Locke's: life there is "solitary, poore, nasty, brutish and short") at least affords the possibility of survival; in fact, "there are many places where they live so now" (1968, 186–7). In contrast, Swift shows the state of nature only to show its impossibility. There can be no such condition as a "state" (in which people continue to live today) because there can be no existence at all outside the human community. Gulliver is indeed far from Crusoe's island, which, despite its initial barreness, is always ready to yield its bounty to individual effort, a self-contained world in which nearly all the material conveniences of society can be supplied by the industry and labor of even a single individual. Life on Gulliver's island is literally unimaginable, a world of barren rock and withering sun that is not only uninviting to the gaze, but repels even the attempt to look upon or envision it:

I considered how impossible it was to preserve my life in so desolate a place, and how miserable my end must be. Yet I found myself so listless and desponding, that I had not the heart to rise and before I could get spirits enough to creep out of my cave, the day was far advanced. I walked a while among the rocks; the day was perfectly clear, and the sun so hot, that I was forced to turn my face from it. (*Prose Works*, Vol. 11, 156).

But the unsurvivable heat and light are suddenly interrupted by the shadow of the flying island, the shadow (and shade) of an irreducible sociability whose mediation alone makes nature liveable. This episode is marginal even to the third voyage because it represents the margins of existence: outside of human society there is only death.

And yet this seemingly insignificant event, destined (as if by design) to be overlooked by readers, is precisely what renders Gulliver's experience comparable (and most directly opposed) to the experience of Robinson Crusoe. Immanent in *Gulliver's Travels* is the notion that for the individual there can be no development *ab initio* (expressed in philosophical form by Descartes and Hobbes, and in literature by Defoe) whether by means of an abstraction from society or a return to a solitude that is posited as original (Marx called such myths "Robinsonades"[6]). The narrative thus conjures up a "state of nature" in which individuals live separate and dissociated existence only to show its impossibility; it denies the notion that individuals are self-sufficient and self-contained and therefore capable of survival in solitude. Swift is led to conclude with Spinoza that

> since fear of solitude exists in all men, because no one in solitude is strong enough to defend himself and procure the necessities of life, it follows that men naturally aspire to the civil state; nor can it happen that men should ever utterly dissolve it. (*A Political Treatise*, VI, 3)

Accordingly, the knowledge that Gulliver acquires during his travels is not primarily a knowledge of the natural world arrived at through his individual sense-experience or the exercise of his reason, a world whose potential yield can be glimpsed by the discerning eye beneath either its apparent barrenness or disorderly profusion. Nor does Gulliver ever demonstrate, as Robinson Crusoe does, the sufficiency of individual reason by (re)inventing a commodious life through observation and the method of trial and error. Gulliver is concerned instead with a description of the customs, practices, morals and religions of the nations he encounters; in short, he is concerned with the reality of human society. And while his observations are the source of part of what he reports, a far more important source, almost entirely absent from Robinson Crusoe's narrative, is the discourse of others. These discourses are often lengthy and detailed, most often presented not in the form of direct quotation but more commonly indirectly, after having been internalized and appropriated by Gulliver. Even when, as in the case of the Brobdingnagian king, Gulliver appears to reject the moral observations he reports, he succeeds only in communicating a truth greater than his own – his very communication reveals the limits and insufficiency of his own intellect. Of course, he is most often not a passive auditor but an active participant in conversations and dialogues that take him far from the opinions with which he entered them, leaving him transformed in ways that he communicates but does not entirely understand or even perceive. His disputations (as they may be called) with the Brobdingnagian king concerning British society leave him exhausted and humiliated. Although he defends his country from the king's criticisms as deftly as his wit allows, his replies "were always turned into ridicule, and I was forced to rest with patience while my noble and most beloved country was so injuriously treated" (*Prose Works* Vol. ii, 133). Even his attempts finally to conceal the "frailties and deformities" of Britain "unfortunately failed of success" (133). Gulliver has thus participated in what can only be called a dialectical experience, a conversation that has forced him to confront the narrow confines of his individual understanding and to begin to transcend its limits to see and to understand what he alone could never know. Gulliver says little that is genuinely original in the sense that the term would take on later in the century: what is marked as important in the narrative is what he repeats from others – their wisdom, their knowledge.

Swift, however, is not simply concerned with discourse: language as such takes on an obvious importance in *Gulliver's Travels*. In clear contrast to Robinson Crusoe, who shows not the slightest inclination to learn the languages of the Indians into whose domain he has been cast, and who forces Friday to communicate with him in English, Gulliver never once imagines any other course for himself than to learn the languages of his hosts. Accordingly, no one speaks pidgin dialects in *Gulliver's Travels* or a permanently disfigured English that would serve to mark the speaker as uncivilized. The same "abrupt propinquity of consonants" that Swift found objectionable in English is intensified to unpronounceable proportions in the languages of the nations he encounters (although this does not serve to identify these languages as inferior). The reader is thus forced to pronounce (or to imagine pronouncing) words like *hlunnh* (the Houyhnhnm word for oats) or *hnhloayn* (the word signifying exhortation) and to share for a moment Gulliver's submission or conformity to a pre-existing linguistic order whose alterity is irreducible. In fact, the Houyhnhnms' speech may be said to be primitive only in the sense that it is pure and uncorrupted. It can do nothing other than communicate what is: it lacks the capacity to prevaricate and evade. It is thus not only from the content, but from the form or structure of these discourses that Gulliver learns, discourses that precede and exceed him.

Yet, the irreducible human sociability that Swift counterposes to the individualism proper to juridical anthropologies exceeds a mere critique of social atomism. It is also a critique of the egalitarianism that is necessary to these doctrines, even if the equality among human beings remains purely formal, a juridical fiction that is never actualized, an original equality that has always already been superseded. For Swift, the sociability proper to humanity takes the form of an organic hierarchy that emerges as a universal: not one nation that Gulliver encounters exhibits an egalitarian form.[7] Thus Swift rejects the Aristotelianism of those who would posit a hierarchy of nations, according to which some are destined to command and others to serve, in favor of what would appear to be a doctrine of the juridical equality of all nations. To this extent he participates in the juridical ideology that he seems otherwise to oppose. But the repressed inequality of nations returns as the hierarchical form internal to every nation. The distance between persons of quality and the lower orders is everywhere the same because the relations of command and obedience are inscribed in nature.

Thus, in Brobdingnag, the petty meanness, selfishness and greed of the farmer who first discovers Gulliver contrasts sharply to the intelligence, generosity and public-spiritedness of the king, and the world of the people with its crowds, diseases and dangers (in Brobdingnag deformities are found where they belong: among the *mobile* whose cancers, goiters and missing limbs provoke disgust) is utterly opposed to the world of the court in which order and wisdom reign. In Laputa, distinctions of social rank are obvious even to a total stranger:

> At my alighting I was surrounded by a crowd of people, those who stood nearest seemed to be of better quality. They beheld me with all the marks and circumstances of wonder, neither indeed was I much in the debt, having never till then seen a race of mortals so singular in their shapes, habits and countenances. Their heads were all reclined either to the right, or the left; one of their eyes turned inward, and the other directly up to the zenith. Their outward garments were adorned with the figures of suns, moons and stars, interwoven with those of fiddles, flutes harps, trumpets, guitars, harpsichords and many more instruments of music unknown to us here in Europe. I observed many in the habits of servants, with a blown bladder fastened like a flail to the end of a short stick, which they carried in their hands. (159)

Here it is not only by their "habits" that Gulliver can immediately distinguish the different ranks of Laputan society (thus recalling sumptuary laws, as well as the market-driven laws of fashion that replaced them), but by bodily traits. In Laputa, unlike Brobdingnag, it is the people of quality who suffer from outward deformations that directly express the degeneration of their inward parts. They are distracted, capable of gazing upward to the heavens or inward into their own minds, but unable to see directly in front of them. They have thus been rendered unfit to care for themselves or others and are dangerously dependent on "the vulgar, whose thoughts and minds were more disengaged" (160). Hence, the decay of Laputan society whose economy has been ruined by projectors, and by a nobility that has abdicated its natural place of authority in the world.

In the land of the Houyhnhnms, the natural gradations of social rank are even more clearly identifiable; to be precise, they are color-coded (Moreau 1981, 119).

> Among the Houyhnhnms, the white, the sorrel, and the iron-grey were not so exactly shaped as the bay, the dapple-grey and the black; nor born with equal talents of the mind, or a capacity to improve them; and therefore continued always in the condition of servants, without ever aspiring to match out of their own race, which in that country would be reckoned monstrous and unnatural. (*Prose Works* Vol. 11, 256)

Here desire, ability, color and social rank all happily coincide (in the land of the Houyhnhnms, just as the authority of human beings over animals is inverted, so is the relation between black and white). The relations of command and obedience are written in the hearts of the Houyhnhnms who, because they live according to the dictates of nature, cannot reasonably imagine living or acting otherwise.

Even more important perhaps than the natural inequality characteristic of the nations he visits is Gulliver's own reaction to the hierarchy implicit in the first two voyages. In one sense, much of the ironic effect of the first half of the work is produced by Gulliver's unstated but nevertheless very active assumption (an assumption that runs counter to much of what he says) that all men are created equal. His egalitarian presuppositions, however, are utterly at odds with the realities that he encounters. In one sense, of course, Gulliver seems innocent of any egalitarianism: he associates almost exclusively with royalty and nobility, and actively avoids contact with the lower orders (for whom he feels contempt, if not disgust, as noted above). But in another sense, the first half of the work offers a figuration of a hierarchy of being, of command and obedience, of superiority and inferiority that is transparent; no hermeneutic is required to decipher it: there are no kings disguised as beggars, no women of quality masquerading as peasants. There are only those whose inferiority to Gulliver in morality is perfectly expressed by their diminutive size, whereas his moral and intellectual superiors (to take the example of the Brobdingnagian king) are giants whose bodies are adequate to the grandeur of their souls.

If it is true that the Lilliputian world is inferior to that of Gulliver, it is equally true that it offers a portrait of British (and European) society reduced to the essence beneath the appearance, the unstated assumptions that guide the actions of these dominions despite and in opposition to the elaborate justifications that excuse the most odious endeavors. Thus the Emperor of Lilliput does not hesitate to refer to himself as the "delight and terror of the universe", exhibiting a pride that is comically inappropriate to his place in that universe. Similarly, he says what European princes dare only to think (and thus states the truth behind their conduct), that he seeks not only to reduce the neighboring kingdom of Blefuscu to "a province, and governing it by a viceroy" but that in doing so he would become "sole monarch of the whole world" (53). When Gulliver "endeavored to divert him from this design by many arguments drawn from policy as well as justice" (53), the

Emperor determines to seek his "utter destruction" (54). The opposition between policy and justice is an important, if implicit, theme in Gulliver's first voyage. In fact, Lilliputian politics are practiced without reference to the immutable truth of justice and are guided by the imperatives of practice alone in the quest to realize an implacable will to power. Lilliputians, however much Gulliver persists in denying it, recognize only Machiavelli's *verità effettuale*, the practical truth of a world without norms or values, and do not even pay lip service to "what should be" (127). The scandal of this world is that it does not even attempt to cover its ambitions or designs with the cloak of religion or morality. We find, for example, that the Lilliputian court was "under many difficulties concerning" Gulliver (32), and because the cost of maintaining a being of his size was so extravagant, they contemplate killing him. Although it is resolved that his life be spared, justice plays no part in the decision. Instead, his life is spared "because the stench of so large a carcase might produce a plague in the metropolis" (32). The dictates of self-interest alone determine the actions of the Lilliputian court, a fact that Gulliver reports even as he conceals its meaning from himself, adroitly excusing and explaining away the most ruthless actions until he himself is threatened by the politics of policy.

Gulliver, unable to dispense with or ignore the laws of true morality, finds that he has no place in a world where virtue is in fact no more than Machiavelli's *virtu* and where the ability to maneuver, to dance on moving ropes, is the test of greatness. Impeached for petitioning to be excused from reducing the empire of Blefuscu to a province of Lilliput and for his "unwillingness to force the consciences, or destroy the lives and liberties of an innocent people" (55), Gulliver is sentenced to be blinded, "for true reasons of state" (70). He is to "see by the eyes of the ministers, since the greatest princes do no more" (70) which will render him better able to serve Lilliput. For Gulliver, a Socratic figure *malgré lui*, sees what the Lilliputians cannot, and his vision renders him unfit to live among those who, without any knowledge of eternal and immutable morality, are guided only by self-interest and the constraints of practice. In Machiavelli's words, "he must fall to ruin among so many who are not good" (1964, 127). Gulliver is a moral giant among his inferiors; but, as an anomaly in this world and who would thus suffer a fate similar to that of Socrates, he has no choice but to flee.

In contrast, Gulliver is "dwarfed" in Brobdingnag. Its natives are not only his superiors in size, they (or at least the Brobdingnagian nobility) are his superiors in morality and learning as well. The man-mountain, as he was called in Lilliput, becomes "Grildrig" the mannikin or little man. His diminutive stature renders his encounters with even rats, monkeys and wasps perilous and he must rely on his superiors for protection. Brobdingnag is a world in which he experiences utter helplessness. At the same time, Brobdingnag differs markedly from Lilliput as a society. Unlike the kingdom of Lilliput, which is constantly at war with its neighbors, Brobdingnag is "wholly excluded from any commerce with the rest of the world" by virtue of its geography. It is consequently an economically self-sufficient land uncorrupted by the enticements of foreign trade and the commercial and political revolutions that foreign trade engenders. Accordingly, Brobdingnag is a stable agrarian society without a standing army, only a militia made up of farmers and tradesmen and commanded by the nobility and gentry. It admits only those improvements and innovations that are of practical benefit to "agriculture and the mechanical arts" (*Prose Works* Vol. 11, 136). Its laws must be formulated in twenty-two words or less and "to write a comment upon any law is a capital crime" (136). Brobdingnag is clearly a society that "raises no quarrels with nature" and as such stands in marked contrast to Gulliver's England.

Unlike the Lilliputian emperor who is so self-absorbed that he evinces no interest in Gulliver's origins, the king of Brobdingnag questions Gulliver quite closely about British society. From his superior vantage point he is able to see not merely the corruptions of British society (for Gulliver initially presents only the ideal that England has set for itself, without indicating how far its development has taken it from that ideal) but the weaknesses of the political model itself. Taking five audiences with the king, "each of several hours", Gulliver describes the model that is the basis of the actual House of Peers and the House of Commons, together with the courts of justice, and gives the king a brief account of British history. In the sixth audience the king "proposed many doubts, queries and objections, upon every article" (129) of Gulliver's narrative until it is no longer a matter of the distance of the real from the ideal but rather the nature of the ideal itself. Europeans constitute a race unto themselves, albeit "a race of little odious vermin" (132) whose history was an heap of conspiracies, rebellions, murders, massacres, revolutions, banishments, the very worst effects that avarice, faction, hypocrisy, perfidiousness, cruelty, rage, madness, hatred, envy, lust, malice and ambition could produce. (132)

– an accident that emerges from nature but which does not partake of its essence.

Finally, Gulliver hopes to win the king's favor and to regain some of his lost pride by appealing to the king's self-interest. He offers the king the gift of gunpowder and with it the gift of absolute power (and in doing so lowers himself to the level of the Lilliputian emperor). But arguments of policy have no effect on the king who, from his vantage point, thinks of justice alone. He has no use for technical innovations like gunpowder even if it "would have made him absolute master of the lives, liberties and fortunes of his people" (135) and regards Gulliver with contempt for making such a proposal. Gulliver's humiliation is thus completed: he is made to feel small, limited and petty, an inferior among superiors. He is too diminished to live according to the natural dictates of justice alone.

One of the most striking discrepancies between Gulliver's experiences as he reports them and his commentary on these experiences is his refusal to accept the reality of the hierarchical order that emerges by the end of the second voyage. For instead of conveying a sense of humility based on his inferiority to the Brobdingnagians, his stay in Brobdingnag results in an identification with his superiors, which causes him upon his return to England to regard those around him as "so many pygmies" and himself "a giant". It is perhaps to be expected that he would steadfastly resist the recognition that Europeans are "inferior" to the Brobdingnagians in more than size: such a recognition would constitute a blow to his pride. But it must be recalled that he is just as reluctant to accept his own superiority over the Lilliputians. He provides innumerable rationalizations to deny the unalloyed cruelty and greed of the Lilliputians and is fully disillusioned only at the end of the voyage. It appears, then, that Gulliver is prevented by more than pride from seeing the realities that lie before him. For pride is the sin of desiring more than is proper to one's station in a social order that is a continuation of the teleology of nature. But this order itself remains invisible to Gulliver, even when it is exhibited in its most manifest and physical forms. All this is strikingly obvious to the reader even as Gulliver persists in believing that both the Lilliputians and the Brobdingnagians are his equals. His inability or unwillingness to see the unequal order of things is used to great comic effect, as when Gulliver appears to take very seriously the charge of having carried on a sexual relationship with a woman six inches tall, or when, while living in Brobdingnag, he attempts unsuccessfully to jump over a pile of dung. Thus the original equality of human beings, a notion essential to emergent liberalisms, is made to appear *prima facie* absurd, a juridical fiction that is utterly at odds with the visible order of terrestrial things, human as well as non-human.

We can begin to see the politics immanent in *Gulliver's Travels*. None of the hierarchical orders that he encounters is the outcome of an original contract or constitutional moment that founds social hierarchies and marks them as artificial, produced by a moment of consent that permits the supersession of the natural state of individual equality and autonomy. On the contrary, the social order, the differentiation of society into unequal ranks, is natural, original, and to that extent necessary, if the society is to prosper (of course, corruption and degeneration are always possible in nature, as the case of Laputa shows). "Constitution" here means the natural composition of the social body as opposed to the artificial foundation of human law that serves as the absolute origin and highest destiny of a given civil state. This in turn allows us to see the meaning of Swift's critique of the state. While it is true that Swift favors a minimal state, he is far from Locke's notion of a state whose sole function is the preservation of individual abso-lute property. There is nothing anarchistic or libertarian about Swift: he approved of a strongly authoritarian society, but one in which authority was primarily exercised outside the state. In a society whose unequal social organization corresponds to the natural order, institutions appear necessary (there are few institu-tions and barely a state at all in the land of the Houyhnhnms) only to counter external threats and the ever-present possibility of "unnatural" rebellion. The absolutist state (or perhaps despotic state: the Lilliputian emperor is associated with the figure of the Oriental despot) (Lock 1980, 129), far from upholding natural relations of command and obedience, equalized all subjects before the sole authority of the sovereign, and tended to institute a dangerous equality that would end only by undermining all au-thority. Before the king of Luggnagg (a nation in which Gulliver sojourns at the conclusion of his third voyage), even "persons of the highest rank" must crawl upon and lick the floor as they advance (they are distinguished from their inferiors in that for them the floor is cleaned prior to the ceremony). But despotism, whether Asiatic or European, is neither the only nor the dominant threat to the natural authority of the aristocracy and gentry. As the king of Brobdingnag observes, money (and its tendency to dissolve all non-economic relations of dominance and subordination and to introduce social mobility, upwards and downwards, forced and voluntary) corrupts not the free election of the most qualified candidate to the Commons but rather the properly subordinate relation of tenant farmers to their landlords (Kramnick 1968, 206–17):

> He then desired to know ... whether a stranger with a strong purse might not influence the vulgar voters to choose him before their own landlords, or the most considerable gentleman in the neighbourhood. (*Prose Works*, Vol. ii, 129)

The implicit norm here seems far from Gulliver's description of the ideal of a House of Commons whose members are "freely picked and culled out by the people themselves" (128), unless it could be argued that "free" tenants would automatically elect their own landlords. Accordingly, in the Brobdingnagian militia (which Swift contrasts favorably to the British practice of a standing army), "every farmer is under the command of his own landlord, and every citizen under that of the principal men in his own city (138); its commanders are thus "only the nobility and gentry without pay or reward" (138). It is clear that in Brobdingnag the landlord–tenant relation is not a merely economic relation founded on a contract concluded between equals; it is rather the extra-economic inclination of the vulgar to follow their superiors.

What is precisely interesting about the political ideal that takes shape in *Gulliver's Travels*, is that it is not at all a matter of reciprocal duties or obligations (imposed externally through the mechanism of the law) but rather of natural inclinations that arise from the heart. The most notable characteristic of Houyhnhnm society is that its order is not mandated by law but truly desired by all the members of the community who cannot reasonably wish to occupy any rank other than that into which they were born or to perform any other function than that to which they have been assigned by nature. Gulliver's Houyhnhnm master desires to have the meaning of law explained to him "because he thought that reason and nature were sufficient guides for a reasonable animal, as we pretended to be, in showing us what we ought to do and what to avoid"(248). In a similar way, there are no words for government or power in the Houyhnhnm language (244) because their "state" or government consists of a "representative council" that meets for five or six days every four years. There is no need for a state among the inhabitants of this nation, at least according to the modern explanation of the state as "umpire" (to use Locke's expression), mediating between the multitude of individuals whose desires lead them into perpetual conflict and adjudicating their competing claims (Locke 1980, 46–7). No state is necessary to mediate conflicts among the Houyhnhnms: they desire only to fulfill the functions that nature has assigned to them and nature is everywhere the source of order. Further, because "their grand maxim is, to cultivate reason, and to be wholly governed by it" (*Prose Works* Vol. 11, 267), there can arise no differences of religion or politics. There is unanimity without coercion or even persuasion:

> Neither is reason among them a point problematical as with us, where men can argue with plausibility on both sides of a question; but strikes you with immediate conviction; as it must needs do where it is not mingled, obscured, or discoloured by passion and interest. I remember it was with extreme difficulty that I could bring my master to understand the meaning of the word *opinion*, or how a point could be disputable; because reason taught us to affirm or deny only where we are certain; and beyond our knowledge cannot do either. So that controversies, wranglings, disputes, and positiveness in false or dubious propositions are evils unknown among the Houyhnhnms. (267)

There is much in this passage that recalls Swift's attack on the "madness" of the modern philosophers in *A Tale of a Tub*: the natural position of the mind is to think through the "common forms", to live so is to live in a "state of serenity" (1958, 171). It is only when the individual breaks with "common understanding as well as common sense" (171) and attempts to know "things agreed on all hands impossible to be known" (171) and surrenders to private dreams and visions as opposed to public reason that he will succumb to madness. Similarly, the king of Brobdingnag criticizes the British legal system on the grounds that "advocates and orators had liberty to plead in cases manifestly known to be unjust, vexatious or oppressive" (*Prose Works* Vol. 11, 130). He finds it laughable that the state would not enforce a unanimous recognition of what is "manifestly known" not only in matters of law but even more in politics and religion, by outlawing dissent. The king

> laughed at my odd kind of arithmetic (as he was pleased to call it) in reckoning the numbers of our people by a computation drawn from the several sects among us in religion and politics. He said, he knew no reason why those who entertain opinions prejudicial to the public should be obliged to change, or should not be obliged to conceal them. As it was tyranny in any government to require the first, so it was weakness not to enforce the second: for a man may be allowed to keep poisons in his closets, but not to vend them about as cordials. (131)

The reference here is impossible to mistake: the Anglican Church is the true Church, its doctrines are manifestly known to be true; to dissent from its teachings is madness, and in any case ought not to be tolerated. Houyhnhnm reason, which renders controversy and schism impossible, is thus the fantasy of a besieged institution, a remembrance of a past that in fact never existed, a time when the people of England neither had nor desired any other religious doctrine or practice than that of the one true Church. The historical reality, of course, was quite different: the brief moments during which the Anglican Church actually enjoyed a monopoly over religious life were the products of coercion, and as such were both short-lived and succeeded by crises of serious magnitude (the 1630s and 1660–78).

But Houyhnhnm society requires no such expedients to produce what would be an artificial social harmony. There the truth strikes one with immediate conviction, especially the truth of one's proper place in nature's order (society is part of nature and therefore in no way opposed to or separate from it). Yet, if we return to the key passage concerning the naturality of command and obedience whose truth is made visible through color, we discover a curious dissymmetry: we are told what the servant races do not want and do not do. It is their transgression against the order of things that "would be reckoned monstrous and unnatural" (256). But what of their masters? In this passage at least, Swift appears to be more concerned with the disorder that rises from below than that which descends from above, from the desire for an inappropriate social mobility that dissolves the natural bonds of society to the unnatural rebellions that only bring chaos and ruin. It is significant that on his fourth voyage Gulliver, having assumed command of his first ship, is soon the object of a conspiracy on the part of his men. The mutineers seize the ship and set Gulliver on the shores of an unknown land. The voyage to the country of the Houyhnhnms thus begins with precisely the unnatural rebellion that cannot happen in the land of those whose name means "perfection of nature".

The only threat to Houyhnhnm society comes from another species of being which cannot properly be said to belong to the social order at all: the Yahoos. In fact, the political vision of the fourth voyage is subject to a kind of splitting: on the one hand, there are the Houyhnhnms who have no need for government and, on the other, the ungovernable Yahoos (who unlike any other group Gulliver encounters do, in certain respects, resemble humankind in a Hobbesian state of nature).[8] The Yahoos (for which all other living things feel a natural antipathy) "hate one another more than they did any different species of animals" (260). If given a surplus of food, "they will instead of eating peaceably, fall together by the ears, each single one impatient to have all to itself" (260). Further, they make war "without any visible cause; those of one district watching all opportunities to surprise the next before they are prepared. But if they find their project hath miscarried, they return home, and, for want of enemies, engage in what I call a civil war among themselves" (260). The Yahoos have no place in the design of nature. They not only disrupt it; they defile it. Because it is impossible to coexist with the Yahoos, they have become the occasion of the only debate that the Houyhnhnms have ever had: "whether the Yahoos should be exterminated from the face of the earth" (271). At this point, if we take seriously Gulliver's identification of the Yahoos with, if not humanity in general, at least the European variety, we are faced with a stunning contradiction. The philosophy immanent in *Gulliver's Travels* is, as has been shown, a philosophy of natural order and natural community – a refusal, inscribed in the letter of the work, of the theoretical foundations of nascent liberalism. Swift might have posited a human order that Gulliver cannot see, and a place within it that he cannot find; the narrative might have found its resolution in the opposition between an order that Gulliver reports and his individual failure to accept that order, in which case Gulliver's madness only reaffirms the design of the social world as it condemns itself. But such is not the case. By the end of the second voyage, it would seem that Gulliver has all the information necessary to determine his proper place in the order of things. Gulliver appears to be midway between the Lilliputians and the Brobdingnagians, the middle term in a hierarchical order, the existence of which was unknown to him before his voyages. It would seem that Gulliver might have discovered the middle way between the worlds superior and inferior to his own, accepted both his capacities and his limitations and gone on to live in a manner appropriate to the station ascribed to him by nature, as in the manner of Houyhnhnm society. In a certain sense, then, a kind of narrative and thematic closure appears only to be suspended at the end of the second voyage. We know that Book Three was the last to be written and that Swift evidently at one time considered inverting the order of the last two books (Ehrenpreis 1962). Further, Book Three has not only received less critical attention than the other three books, but is generally considered the least coherent and unified. Without accepting the norms of unity and coherence that such critics have attempted to impose on *Gulliver's Travels*, we may nevertheless acknowledge the existence of something like a caesura or a gap that divides the work between the second and third voyages. The closure that might be expected to follow the complementary experiences of Lilliput and Brobdingnag is never achieved.

The third and fourth voyages mark precisely the denaturalization of humanity. This denaturalization might have led Swift, as it did Hobbes, to a corresponding disordering of nature, to an evacuation of original purposes and ultimate ends from the natural world. But to proceed to such a world-view, to question the notion of a providential order, would be to give way to the atheistic and materialist tendencies of contemporary philosophy and its visions of a world without design or eternal and immutable justice (in short, the Lilliputian world-view). Accordingly, Swift's inability or unwillingness to determine the place appointed to humanity in the providential order so essential to Anglican ideology is combined with a refusal to call that order into question, a defense which consists of a refusal to allow the recognition of a disordered humanity to undermine the vision of a cosmic order, to contain this recognition, to seal it off and prevent it from contaminating the Anglican world-view. Swift's "solution" to this problem is radical. In order to defend Anglican theology against the evidence of history and personal experience, it is no longer enough to declare humanity corrupt; humanity must be declared monstrous and unnatural, a freak species, or *lusus naturae* (*Prose Works* Vol. 11, 104) for which there is no place in the plenitude of nature. In this sense, the narrative exhibits the becoming-monstrous of humanity.

As early as the second voyage the notion emerges of the un-naturalness of humanity. Shortly after his arrival in Brobdingnag, Gulliver is examined by "three great scholars" on the orders of the king. He reports that

> they all agreed that I could not be produced according to the regular laws of nature, because I was not framed with a capacity of preserving my life, either by swiftness, or climbing of trees, or digging holes in the earth. They observed by my teeth, which they viewed with great ex-actness, that I was a carnivorous animal; yet most quadrupeds being an overmatch for me, and field mice, with some others too nimble, they could not imagine how I should be able to support my self, unless I fed upon snails and other insects, which they offered by many learned arguments to evince that I could not possibly do.... After much debate they concluded unanimously that I was only *relplum scalath*, which is interpreted literally, *lusus naturae*; a determination exactly agreeable to the modern philosophy of Europe, whose professors, disdaining the old evasion of occult causes, whereby the followers of Aristotle endeav-our in vain to disguise their ignorance, have invented this wonderful solution of all difficulties to the unspeakable advancement of human knowledge. (104)

In one sense, of course, the conclusion reached by the three Brobdingnagian scholars is laughable. When they decide that Gulliver could not possibly represent a previously unknown spe-cies but must be a singular freak of nature, an accidental outcome of the regular workings of nature, the reader laughs, not only at their ignorance, but at their presumption as well. Further, their conclusion identifies them with modern European scholars who, rather than improving on the findings of the followers of Aristotle, have simply devised new means (this time natural rather than supernatural) of disguising their ignorance. These themes are explored in greater detail in his next voyage when Gulliver en-counters the Grand Academy of Lagado. But at the same time, the Brobdingnagians' error in judgment introduces new themes which, instead of inviting the reader to join in the laughter at the ignorance of those "others", rather turn the joke on the Europeans themselves. For the fact that Gulliver is a member of a species and not a freak of nature does not negate the scholars' observations on the inadequacy of his frame, and more generally on the difficulty of finding a place for him in the order of things. It simply prepares the way for the king's denunciation of the "pernicious race" of which Gulliver is a member as the most "odious vermin that nature ever suffered to crawl upon the surface of the earth" (132).

Near the end of his stay in Brobdingnag, Gulliver discovers a treatise on morality and devotion which "treats of the weakness of human kind" (137). Its author showed in the "manner of the European moralists" (of whom Swift was known to approve)

> how diminutive, contemptible and helpless an animal was man in his own nature; how unable to defend himself from the inclemencies of the air or the fury of wild beasts ... He argued that the laws of nature absolutely required that we should have been made, in the beginning of a size more large and robust, not so liable to destruction from every little accident of a tile falling from an house, or a stone cast from the hand of a boy, or of being drowned in a little brook. (139)

Or falling into a pile of dung or being seized by a monkey. Gulliver, however, refuses the "discontent" that the work expresses, dismissing it as derived "from the quarrels we raise with nature" (137), without any recognition that he himself has experienced what the Brobdingnagian moralist has described, and that if the Brobdingnagians are "diminutive, contemptible and helpless", how much more so must the Europeans be. It is not only his insistence on his equality to the Brobdingnagians that makes Gulliver appear absurd, it is also his refusal to see how "contemptible" the Europeans are.

Gulliver only comes to see the truth of his race and the causes of its degeneration during his stay among the sorcerers of Glubbdubdrib. There, he is freed from the world of appearances, which vanishes "like visions in a dream, when we wake on a sudden" (194), and is permitted to see into the essence of things. From the first, he is confronted with the decay of the race, with the fact that the ancients placed next to the moderns appear almost to be a different order of being:

> I desired that the senate of Rome might appear before me in one large chamber, and a modern representative in counterview in another. The

first seemed to be an assembly of heroes and demigods; the other a knot of pedlars, pickpockets, highwaymen and bullies. (195–6)

The explanation for the historical degeneration of the assembly into a knot, and heroes into pedlars is a purely physical one: the lineages of royal and noble families, the purity of which ought to have been guarded with the utmost care, have been contaminated with an infusion of impure blood. When Gulliver desires to see "eight or nine generations" of certain royal families, he is surprised to see that in every case the hereditary line is interrupted with fiddlers, barbers, and various members of the Roman clergy (198). In the case of noble families, the base characteristics which are handed down from generation to generation are the result either of ancestors bringing "the pox into a noble house, which hath lineally descended in scrofulous tumors to their posterity", or of the "interruption of lineages by pages, lackeys, valets, coachmen, gamesters, fiddlers, players, captains, and pickpockets" (198–9). Thus, if the modern nobility have abdicated the social place proper to them, and advocate policies that directly undermine the landed interest that Swift thought was naturally their own, it is because they are not the nobility at all, but descendants of their "ancestors'" servants and tenants. Disease and corruption have thus "levelled" European society. Gulliver has made the tragic discovery that he (and the entire polity with him) no longer has any true superiors:

> I hope I may be pardoned if these discoveries inclined me a little to abate that profound veneration which I am naturally apt to pay to persons of high rank, who ought to be treated with the utmost respect due to their sublime dignity, by us their inferiors. (200)

He concludes by reflecting on a general humanity without distinction or degree,

> how much the race of human kind was degenerate among us, within these hundred years past. How the pox under all its consequences and denominations had altered every lineament of an English countenance, shortened the size of bodies, unbraces the nerves, relaxed the sinews and muscles, introduced a sallow complexion, and rendered the flesh loose and rancid. (201)

For the Houyhnhnms, the very existence of the Yahoos raises unanswerable questions. As Gulliver's master examines him, he observes that not one part of his body appears to answer to the requirement for which it was certainly designed (and in this repeats the arguments of the Brobdingnagian scholars). His feet are "too soft to bear the ground" (242). As a biped, he is in constant danger of falling. His face is organized in such a way that he could not look on either side without turning his head (242). But perhaps most striking is the "natural antipathy which every creature discovered against us" (243). The European Yahoos have been able to compensate for their natural deficiencies by employing reason to invent artificial supplements (clothes, weapons, and so on) to allow them not simply to survive but to prosper. The very use of reason, however, has only made the Yahoo race more alien to nature's order. Gulliver reports that his master

> looked upon us as a sort of animal to whose share, by what accident he could not conjecture, some small pittance of reason had fallen whereof we made no other use than by its assistance to aggravate our natural corruptions, and to acquire new ones which nature had not given us. (259)

Thus, when Gulliver describes the propensity for war among European princes, the Houyhnhnm master fears that he has "said the thing which is not" given that "nature hath left you uncapable of doing much mischief" (247). Gulliver responds with a torrent of descriptions to show that the artificial means of doing mischief have so far outstripped anything that nature has yet devised, that as many as a million Yahoos may perish in the course of a single war, and that battles in which "dead bodies drop down in pieces from the clouds" are beheld "to the great diversion of all the spectators" (247). And yet the rationality that has produced weapons of mass destruction serves only the malice and not the well-being of the European Yahoos. The rule of law (the greatest expression of human reason according to other philosophers of the eighteenth century) is nothing more than a "confederacy of injustice", allowing some to injure others for gain or merely for spite.

But, most, it is the introduction of money, originally intended as an emolument for trade (and therefore as rational way of securing the diffusion of goods and labor) that has completed the corruption of Gulliver's native land. First, it has ruined the nobility and produced an unnatural levelling of society:

our young noblemen are bred from their childhood in idleness and luxury; that as soon as the years will permit, they consume their vigor and contract odious diseases among lewd females; and when their fortunes are almost ruined, they marry some woman of mean birth, disagreeable person, and unsound constitution, merely for the sake of money, whom they hate and despise... The productions of such marriages are generally scrofulous, ricketty, or deformed children, by which means the family seldom continues above three generations. (256)

Money allows those without privilege of birth or ability (except the ability to accumulate money) to possess estates, noble wives, and even titles. It has instituted an artificial, monstrous hierarchy that has ruined a green and pleasant land, reducing the multitudes to poverty "to make a few live plentifully" (251). The food and drink produced at home are sold abroad to the highest bidder, while many must beg for their daily bread.

Thus European society (at least in modern times) becomes a kind of disease for which there is no cure (except perhaps the radical one of extermination) and which is destined to progress to an apocalyptic end. If Gulliver has discovered at the conclusion of his travels the providential design that shapes this world, the principles of its perfection, he has simultaneously discovered that he (and his kind) have no place in its order. This "discovery" is obviously a defence, a way of preventing the recognition that the world is no longer intelligible from the point of view of Swift's political philosophy, from calling that philosophy into question, from suggesting that it might be inadequate to the world that it purports to explain. This, then, is Swift's "solution" to the discrepancy between the spontaneous philosophy of the Anglican Church and the historical reality that confronted it. If the world of eighteenth-century Britain is utterly at odds with the social vision of Anglican Aristotelianism, it is not because that vision is in any way inadequate or outworn, but because that world is exogenous to the eternal and immutable order that is the sole concern of the Church. European society is thus made monstrous in order to save the doctrines (and the institution that they justify) to which it so little corresponds. If Anglican philosophy can no longer explain the human world, it is the world that is wrong, a freak, a monster, an accidental product of the regular workings of nature, without purpose or end. The society of humankind is thus not to be explained but denounced: its history is nothing more than its corruption, its progress the progress of a disease called (European) humanity.

But what of Gulliver? Have we not been warned by several generations of critics not to confuse his views with those of Swift, to regard him as the most unreliable of narrators whose statements cause us to laugh at, as often as with, him? There is no question that by the end of the work it is impossible any longer to identify with Gulliver. The question is rather how and why we as readers begin gradually (or is it gradually?) to withdraw our identification. In any case, it is certainly not because of his "misanthropy", the absurdity of which is self-evident according to some readers. Too many have been taken in for this simply to be a misreading. It is rather that Gulliver's final condemnation of the human world is simultaneously a condemnation of himself. And for good reason: Gulliver's aversion to humanity has been acted out, but not reflected upon, by him from the beginning of the work.

Thus his final reunion with his family who received him "with great surprise and joy" fills him "only with hatred, disgust and contempt" (289). As he approaches his house, Gulliver thinks "that by copulating with one of the Yahoo species I had become parent of more" and is struck "with the utmost shame, confusion and horror" (289). His wife then takes him into her arms and kisses him, but "having not been used to the touch of that odious animal for so many years", he falls "in a swoon for almost an hour" (289). These responses clearly mark Gulliver as unnatural and monstrous himself: he not only lacks the natural inclination for the opposite sex (that since Plato and Aristotle has been regarded as the hallmark of human sociability), but his desire has been replaced by aversion. Likewise, the sight of his family only inspires "horror". Love for the opposite sex and love for one's children were simply the most primitive manifestations of the natural sociability of which no traces may any longer be found in Gulliver. But were they ever to be found? Gulliver not only repeatedly abandons his family over a fifteen-year period, evincing little interest in their welfare, but, with the exception of the malicious rumor of his affair with the Lilliputian lady, there is no hint of sexual intrigue or feeling at all except aversion. The image of a nurse suckling a child (and breasts in general) in Brobdingnag is regarded with more disgust than Gulliver has ever felt. Breasts are "dugs", "monstrous" not simply by virtue of the size (although even the breasts of female Yahoos "often reached almost to the ground as they walked") (223) but even more because the breast suggests that dependence of child on mother that most of the societies that Gulliver encounters seek to suppress or deny. Finally, a naked Gulliver, bathing in a stream, is embraced "after a most fulsome manner" (267) by a female Yahoo, confirming at once his membership and hatred of that pernicious race. But there is no greater confirmation of his being a Yahoo than the natural antipathy he feels for his own kind: Gulliver is a living repudiation of the sociability Swift thought proper to humankind.

Finally, at the conclusion of his wanderings, Gulliver has rejected family and society, living among his "own" as he once lived among others, a stranger. He finds that there is no other place for him than among those he cannot tolerate. Not because it is his proper place but because it is the place for those for whom there is no proper place. We can hardly identify with Gulliver, but at the same time are powerless not to. Left to vacillate without conclusion between the positions of the fool and the knave, we may know that we have shared, if only for the hours it takes us to read *Gulliver's Travels*, the historical despair of a Church of England man before the deserts of the present and the infinite abysses of the future.

Notes

1. "All the Contradictions of a Poisoned Age"

1. This is not to say that Ehrenpreis's work is not immensely valuable: on the contrary, it is an indispensable tool for anyone who would undertake the task of truly reading Swift.

2. I have followed Edward Said's suggestion that the proper way to read Swift is to "accept the discontinuities he experienced in the way he experienced them: as either actual or imminent losses of tradition, heritage, position, history, losses located at the center of his disjointed verbal production. And this acceptance is not so much a psychological as it is a set of conditions that makes the whole range of Swift's psychology possible, from a concern with 'fair liberty' to an excremental fixation" (1984, 65).

3. I refer of course to the thesis of J.H. Plumb's *The Growth of Political Stability in England, 1675–1725*. This thesis has recently been contested, notably by J.C.D. Clark in *Rebellion and Revolution* (1986) and Linda Colley in *In Defiance of Oligarchy* (1982). While Clark argues that instability persisted until 1832, Colley argues that stability had already been achieved by the end of the reign of Charles II. For reasons that lie beyond the scope of this work, I find their arguments unconvincing.

4. These reference points were central to Tory doctrine in general, especially in the years following the defeat of 1714 (Colley 1982). The English Civil War in particular became a site of interpretive conflict. The importance for Swift's work of early-eighteenth-century debates about the revolution of the 1640s has not been sufficiently noted.

5. Even his pamphlets on the Irish economy were connected to the Church of Ireland's financial state. The woolen question directly affected the Anglican landlords whose financial well-being was essential to the Church (McCracken 1986).

6. Swift not only supported the penal laws but knew very well that the liberation of the Irish people would be his undoing:

> if we were under any real fear of the papists in this kingdom, it would be hard to think us so stupid, as not to be equally apprehensive with *others*, since we are likely to be the greatest and more immediate suffer-

ers; but, on the contrary, we look upon them to be altogether as inconsiderable as the women and children. Their lands are almost entirely taken from them, and they are rendered uncapable of puchasing any more; and for the little that remains, Provision is made by the late Act against Popery, that it will daily crumble away: To prevent which, some of the most considerable among them are already turned Protestants, and so, in all Probability, will many more. Then, the Popish Priests are all registered, and without Permission (which, I hope, will not be granted) they can have no Successors ... The common people, without Discipline, or natural Courage, being little better than *Hewers of wood, and Drawers of Water*, are out of all capacity of doing any mischief (*Prose Works* Vol. 2, 120).

One of the few literary historians even to address the contradiction inherent in Swift's claim to speak for "the whole people of Ireland" is Carole Fabricant in her *Swift's Landscape* (1982). In her otherwise highly original and illuminating study, however, Fabricant appears to endorse the notion of a unity of interest between the colonizer and the colonized, which, whatever Swift's subjective grasp of the historical reality, is untenable. Even Laura Brown, whose (1993) study directly concerns the question of empire, fails to see the irony of Swift's anti-colonialism. Swift's Ireland was the first model of the apartheid state and he very directly benefited from the institutional oppression of the Irish people (an oppression, moreover, that was founded and constantly maintained by the might of the British military).

7. For a classic statement of the notion of the "unfinished revolution", see Perry Anderson's early "Origins of the Present Crisis" (in Anderson 1992). His later "The Notion of Bourgeois Revolution" (in 1992) offers a more complex view.

8. On Atterbury in particular and the period in general, especially as it shaped Church–State relations, see G.V. Bennett (1975).

9. Although it is important to note, as Landa (1954) reminds us, that even Swift's concerns with the economic condition of Ireland had everything to do with the fiscal condition of the Church of Ireland.

10. As Swift never tired of pointing out, the Whig charges against the Church as an instrument of absolute power in the 1680s were untenable, given that James II saw the Church as an obstacle to the absolutist state.

11. See Christopher Hill's classic account, *The World Turned Upside Down* (1972), as well as Brian Manning's *The English People and the English Revolution* (1991).

12. Thus Swift singles out the issue of Charles's taxation without parliamentary approval as the one injustice he committed during his reign. Taxation was, of course, *the* political issue of the Tory opposition after 1714. This time it was blamed on a corrupt oligarchy instead of the monarch directly.

13. Landa (1954) notes that Swift regarded Henry VIII as the source of "the weakness and poverty of the Church" (161). See especially Swift's marginalia (*Prose Works* Vol. 5, 247–51).

14. E.P. Thompson refers to the Church of England as "that extraordinary hybrid creature" (1993, 378).

15. For the various Anglican arguments advanced to justify the swearing of allegiance to William and Mary, see F.P. Lock, *Swift's Tory Politics* (1983), Ch. 2.

2. A Perpetual War

1. For an account of the Ancient–Moderns controversy in general, see Joseph M. Levine (1991). For a discussion of the particular debate involving Swift, see Starkman (1950); Ehrenpreis (1962) Vol. I, 226–37; Bennett (1975) 38–43.

2. It is sometimes said that Swift lacked any real interest in philosophy. The contents of his library indicate otherwise. He owned the collected works of Plato, Aristotle and Spinoza. He owned individual works by, among others, Lucretius, Pascal (*Pensées*), Descartes, Malebranche, Hobbes (heavily annotated editions of *Leviathan* and *De Cive*), Grotius, Pufendorf, Locke (political works), Bodin, and Richard Simon (Williams, in Swift 1963).

3. I have borrowed the title of this section from Donald Ver Hey, *The Madness of Method* (Ph.D. dissertation, Ohio University, 1973).

4. Quarrels with Nature

1. For an account of the early commentaries on *Gulliver's Travels*, see Bertrand A. Goldgar, "Gulliver's Travels and the Opposition to Walpole" (1970).

2. For an overview of the controversy, see James L. Clifford, "Gulliver's Fourth Voyage: 'Hard' and 'Soft' Schools of Interpretation" (1974).

3. Étienne Balibar's *Citizen Subject* (1991) provides an exceptionally comprehensive analysis of the transition from the "world of subjection" to the "world of right".

4. Suarez also defended the rights of Catholic subjects under Protestant monarchs with absolutist pretensious. His *Defensio Fidei Catholicae, Et Apostolicae Adversus Anglicannae Sectae Errores* (1613) was a response to James I's polemics against the jurisdiction of the papacy.

5. Louis Sala-Molins shows that the European Enlightenment cannot be fully comprehended unless one understands that the slave trade was not only not an exception to it but was fully integrated into its theory and practice. See his *Les misères des lumières. Sous la raison, l'outrage.*

6. In the *Grundrisse*, Marx begins his critique of the methodological individualism of eighteenth-century economic theory thus:

The individual and isolated hunter and fisherman, with whom Smith and Ricardo begin, belongs to the unimaginative conceits of the eighteenth-century Robinsonades, which in no way express merely a reaction against over-sophistication and a return to a misunderstood natural life, as cultural historians imagine ... Smith and Ricardo still stand with both feet on the shoulders of the eighteenth-century prophets, in whose imaginations this eighteenth-century individual – the product on the one side of the dissolution of the feudal forms of society, and on the other, of the new forces of production developed since the sixteenth century – appears as an ideal, whose existence they project into the past. Not as a historic result but as history's point of departure. As the Natural Individual appropriate to their notion of human nature, not arising historically, but posited by nature. (1973, 83)

7. Moreau notes that one of the central orgainizing principles of the utopian literature of the period (of which *Gulliver's Travels* is clearly not an example) is the notion of "the equality of citizens as legal subjects (*sujets de droit*) (1981, 131).

8. The contrast between the Houyhnhnms and the Yahoos resembles Hobbes's discussion (in Chapter 17 of *Leviathan*) of the differences between naturally sociable animals whose private interest coincides with the common good, and humanity whose desires are never satisfied, who seek what others have irrespective of need, and who know how to lie (1968, 225–6).

Bibliography

Althusser, Louis. "On Tendencies in Philosophy". *Essays in Self-Criticism*. London: New Left Books, 1976.
———— *Lenin and Philosophy*. New York: Monthly Review Press, 1971.
———— *Philosophy and the Spontaneous Philosophy of the Scientists*. London: Verso, 1989.
———— *Politics & History*. London: New Left Books, 1972.
Anderson, Perry. "Origins of the Present Crisis" and "The Notion of Bourgeois Revolution". *English Questions*. London: Verso, 1992.
———— *Lineages of the Absolutist State*. London: New Left Books, 1974.
Aquinas, Thomas. *The Summa Theologica*. 61 volumes. New York: McGraw-Hill, 1964.
Aristotle. *Metaphysics*. Oxford: The Clarendon Press, 1924.
———— *Nicomachean Ethics*. Oxford: The Clarendon Press, 1925.
———— *Politics*. New York: The Modern Library, 1943.
———— *Posterior Analytics*. Oxford: The Clarendon Press, 1975.
———— *Topics*. Paris: les Belles lettres, 1967.
Arnauld, Antoine, and Pierre Nicole. *La Logique ou l'art de penser*. Paris: Flammarion, 1970.
Aubenque, Pierre. *Le problème de l'être chez Aristote*. Paris: Presses Universitaires de France, 1962.
Balibar, Étienne. *Spinoza et la politique*. Paris: Presses Universitaires de France, 1985.
———— "Spinoza the Anti-Orwell". *Rethinking Marxism* 2.3, 1989.
———— *Citizen Subject*. In *Who Comes After the Subject?*, edited by Eduardo Cadava, Peter Connor, and Jean-Luc Nancy. New York: Routledge, 1991.
Bennett, G.V. *The Tory Crisis in Church and State*. Oxford: Clarendon Press, 1975.
Bentley, Richard. "The Folly of Atheism". *The Works of Richard Bentley*, *D.D.* 4 vols. London: T. Macpherson, 1838.
Bloch, Olivier Rene. *La philosophie de Gassendi*. The Hague: Martinus Nijhoff, 1971.
Brown, Laura. *Ends of Empires*. Ithaca: Cornell University Press, 1993.

Brown, Norman O. *Life Against Death*. Middletown: Wesleyan University Press, 1959.

Burtt, E.A. *The Metaphysical Foundations of Modern Science*. New York: Harcourt, Brace & Co., 1927.

Bury, J.B. *The Idea of Progress*. New York: Dover, 1932.

Canguilhem, Georges. *La formation du réflexe aux XVIIe et XVIIIe siècles*. Paris: Vrin, 1977.

Carnochan, W.B. *Lemuel Gulliver's Mirror for Man*. Berkeley: University of California Press, 1968.

Clark, J.C.D. *Rebellion and Revolution*. New York: Cambridge University Press, 1986.

Clark, John R. *Form and Frenzy in Swift's Tale of a Tub*. Ithaca: Cornell University Press, 1970.

Clifford, James L. "Gulliver's Fourth Voyage: 'Hard' and 'Soft' Schools of Interpretation". In *Quick Spings of Sense: Studies in the Eighteenth Century*, edited by Larry S. Champion. Athens: University of Georgia Press, 1974.

Colie, Rosalie L. "Spinoza in England, 1665–1730". *Proceedings of the American Philosophical Society* 107.3 (1963).

Colley, Linda. *In Defiance of Oligarchy: The Tory Party 1715–1760*. Cambridge: Cambridge University Press, 1982.

Cross, Claire. *Church and People 1450–1660*. Atlantic Highlands: Humanities Press, 1976.

Cudworth, Ralph. *The True Intellectual System of the Universe*. 3 vols. London: Thomas Tegg, 1845.

Davis, Brion David. *The Problem of Slavery in Western Culture*. Ithaca: Cornell University Press, 1966.

Defoe, Daniel. *A Tour Through the Whole Island of Great Britain*. New York: Dutton, 1962.

Deleuze, Gilles. *Expressionism in Philosophy: Spinoza*. New York: Zone Books, 1990.

Descartes, René. *The Philosophical Writings of Descartes*. 2 vols. Cambridge: Cambridge University Press, 1985.

Downie, J.A. "Swift's Politics". In *Proceedings of the First Munster Symposium on Jonathan Swift*, edited by J. Hermann and Heinz J. Vienken. Munich: Fink, 1985.

Ehrenpreis, Irvin. *Swift: the Man, his Works and the Age*. 3 vols. Cambridge: Harvard University Press, 1962.

Empson, William. *Some Versions of Pastoral*. New York: New Directions, 1935.

Fabricant, Carole. *Swift's Landscape*. Baltimore: Johns Hopkins University Press, 1982.

Fontenelle, Bernard. "Digression sur les Anciens et les Modernes". *Oeuvres*. Paris, 1818.

Gankroger, Stephen, ed. *Descartes: Philosophy, Mathematics and Physics*. Sussex: Harvester Press, 1980.

Gargani, Aldo G. *Hobbes e la scienza*. Turin: Giulio Einaudi, 1971.
Gassendi, Pierre. *The Selected Works of Pierre Gassendi*. New York: Johnson Reprint, 1972.
Gilson, Étienne. *Études sur le rôle de la pensée médiévale dans la formation du système cartesien*. Paris: Vrin, 1930.
————— *History of Christian Philosophy in the Middle Ages*. New York: Random House, 1955.
————— *Jean Duns Scot*. Paris: Vrin, 1952.
Goldgar, Bertrand A. "Gulliver's Travels and the Opposition to Walpole". In *The Augustan Milieu*, edited by Henry Knight Miller. London: Oxford University Press, 1970.
Grotius, Hugo. *De Iure Praedae Commentarius*, edited by James Brown Scott. Oxford: Clarendon Press, 1950.
Gueroult, Martial. *Descartes' Philosophy Interpreted According to the Order of his Reasons: Vol. I The Soul and God*. Minneapolis: University of Minnesota Press, 1984.
Gwatkin. *Church and State in England to the Death of Queen Anne*. London: Longmans, Green and Co., 1917.
Hanke, Lewis. *Aristotle and the American Indians*. Chicago: Henry Regnery Company, 1959.
Harth, Phillip. *Swift and Anglican Rationalism*. Chicago: University of Chicago Press, 1961.
Hill, Christopher. *The World Turned Upside Down*. London: Temple & Smith, 1972.
————— "A Bourgeois Revolution?" In *Three British Revolutions: 1641, 1688, 1776*, edited by J.G.A. Pocock. Princeton: Princeton University Press, 1980.
Hobbes, Thomas. *Leviathan*, edited by C.B. Macpherson. Harmondsworth: Penguin, 1968.
————— *Body, Man and Citizen*. New York: Collier, 1962.
————— *Vita*. London, 1679.
Hooker, Richard. *Of the Laws of Ecclesiastical Polity*. 2 vols. London: Everyman, 1969.
Jacobs, Margaret C. *The Newtonians and the English Revolution 1689–1720*. Ithaca: Cornell University Press, 1976.
Johnson, Samuel. *Lives of the Poets*. 3 vols. Oxford: Clarendon Press, 1905.
Johnston, Edith Mary. *Ireland in the Eighteenth Century*. Dublin: Gill and Macmillan, 1974.
Jones, J.R. *The Revolution of 1688 in England*. New York: Norton, 1972.
————— *Country and Court*. London: Edward Arnold, 1978.
Jones, Richard Foster. *Ancients and Moderns*. St. Louis: Washington University Press, 1936
Koyré, Alexandre. *From the Closed World to the Infinite Universe*. Baltimore: Johns Hopkins University Press, 1957.
————— *Newtonian Studies*. Chicago: University of Chicago Press, 1965.

Kramnick, Isaac. *Bolingbroke and his Circle*. Ithaca: Cornell University Press, 1968.

Landa, Louis. *Swift and the Church of Ireland*. Oxford: Clarendon Press, 1954.

Leff, Gordon. *Medieval Thought*. Harmondsworth: Penguin Books, 1958.

Levine, Joseph M. *The Battle of the Books: History and Literature in Augustan Age*. Ithaca: Cornell University Press, 1991.

Lock, F.P. *The Politics of Gulliver's Travels*. Oxford: Clarendon Press, 1980.

———— *Swift's Tory Politics*. London: Duckworth, 1983.

Locke, John. *Essay Concerning Human Understanding*. New York: Oxford University Press, 1987.

———— *Second Treatise of Government*. Indianapolis: Hackett Publishing Company, 1980.

Lucretius Carus, Titus. *De Rerum Natura*. Cambridge: Harvard University Press, 1975.

Macherey, Pierre. *Hegel ou Spinoza*. Paris: Maspero, 1979.

———— *A Theory of Literary Production*. London: Routledge, 1978.

Machiavelli. *The Prince*. Trans. Mark Musa. New York: St. Martin's Press 1964.

Manning, Brian. *The English People and the English Revolution*. London: Bookmarks, 1991.

Marx, Karl. *Grundrisse*. New York: Vintage, 1973.

McCracken, J.L. "Protestant Ascendancy and the Life of Colonial Nationalism, 1714–60". In *A New History of Ireland*, Vol. IV, edited by T.W. Moody. Oxford: Clarendon Press, 1986.

Milhaud, Gaston. *Descartes savant*. Paris: F. Alcan, 1921.

Mintz, Thomas. *The Hunting of Leviathan*. Cambridge: Cambridge University Press, 1969.

Montag, Warren. "Swift and the Materialist Tradition". Ph.D. dissertation. Claremont Graduate School, 1989.

More, Henry. *Enthusiasmus Triumphatus*, London, 1656.

———— *The Philosophical Writings of Henry More*. New York: Oxford University Press, 1925.

Moreau, Pierre-François. *Spinoza*. Paris: Editions du Seuil, 1975.

———— *Le récit utopique droit naturel et roman de l'état*. Paris: Presses Universitaires de France, 1981.

Negri, Antonio. *The Savage Anomaly*. Minneapolis: University of Minnesota Press, 1991.

Nicholson, Marjorie Hope. "The Early Stage of Cartesianism in England". *Studies in Philology* 26 (1929).

Pagden, Anthony. *Spanish Imperialism and the Political Imagination*. New Haven: Yale University Press, 1990.

Pascal, Blaise. *Pensées*. Baltimore: Penguin Books, 1966.

Paulson, Ronald. *Theme and Structure in Swift's Tale of a Tub*. New Haven: Yale University Press, 1960.

Plato. *Collected Dialogues*, edited by Edith Hamilton and Hamilton Cairns. Princeton: Princeton University Press, 1961.

Plumb, J.H. *The Growth of Political Stability in England, 1675–1725*. London: Macmillan, 1967.

Quintana, Ricardo. *The Mind and Art of Jonathan Swift*. London: Oxford University Press, 1936.

Rai, Milan. "Columbus in Ireland". *Race & Class* 34.4 (1993).

Rolston, Bill. "The Training Ground: Ireland, Conquest and Decolonisation". *Race & Class*. 34.4 (1993).

Rosenheim, Edward W. "Swift and the Martyred Monarch." *Philological Quarterly*. 54 (1975).

———— "Swift's *Ode to Sancroft*: Another Look". *Modern Philology* 73 (1976).

Ross, John F. *Swift and Defoe*: A Study in Relationship. Berkeley: University of California Press, 1941.

Said, Edward. "Swift's Tory Anarchy". *The World, the Text, and the Critic*. London: Faber and Faber, 1984.

Sala-Molins, Louis. *Les misères et les lumières. Sous la raison, l'outrage*. Paris: Robert Laffont, 1992.

Sarasohn, Lisa T. "Motion and Morality: Pierre Gassendi, Thomas Hobbes and the Mechanical World-View". *Journal of the History of Ideas* 46.3 (1985).

Simms, J.G. *Colonial Nationalism: 1692–1776*. Cork: The Mercier Press, 1976.

———— "Protestant Ascendancy, 1691-1714". In *A New History of Ireland Vol. IV*, edited by T.W. Moody. Oxford: Clarendon Press, 1986.

Smith, Frederick N. *Language and Reality in Swift's Tale of a Tub*. Columbus: Ohio State University.

Spinoza, Baruch. *The Collected Works of Spinoza*, edited by Edwin Curley. Princeton: Princeton University Press, 1985.

———— *A Theological-Political Treatise and A Political Treatise*. New York: Dover, 1951.

Spragens, Thomas A., Jr. *The Politics of Motion*. Lexington: University Press of Kentucky, 1973.

Starkman, Mirian Kosh. *Swift's Satire on Learning in a Tale of a Tub*. Princeton: Princeton University Press, 1950.

Suarez, Francisco S.J. *Selections From Three Works. De Legibus, Ac Deo Legislatore*, 1612; *Defensio Fidei Catholicae, Et Apostolicae Adversus Anglicannae Sectae Errores*, 1613; *De Triplici Virtute Theologica, Fide, Spe, Et Charitate*, 1621. 2 vols. Oxford: Clarendon Press, 1944.

Swift, Jonathan. *A Tale of a Tub*, edited by A.C. Guthkelch and D. Nichol Smith. Oxford: Clarendon Press, 1958.

———— *The Correspondence of Jonathan Swift*, edited by Harold Williams. 4 Volumes. Oxford: Clarendon Press, 1963.

———— *The Battle of the Books*, edited by A. Guthkelch. London: Chatto & Windus, 1908.

———— *The Prose Works of Jonathan Swift*. 16 vols, edited by Herbert Davis. London: G. Bell, 1897–1925.

Temple, William. *Essays on Ancient and Modern Learning*. Oxford: The Clarendon Press, 1909.

Thompson, E.P. "The Making of a Ruling Class". *Dissent*, Summer 1993.

———— "Eighteenth-Century English Society: Class Struggle without Class?" *Social History* 3.2 (1978).

Tosel, André, *Spinoza ou le crépuscule de la servitude*. Paris: Aubier, 1984.

Tuck, Richard. *Natural Rights Theories: Their origin and development*. Cambridge: Cambridge University Press, 1979.

Van Leeuwen, Henry G. *The Problem of Certainty in English Thought 1630–1690*. The Hague: Martinus Nijhoff, 1963.

Ver Hey, Donald. "The Madness of Method". Ph.D. dissertation, Ohio University, 1973.

Vernière, Paul. *Spinoza et la pensée française avant la révolution*. Paris: Presses Universitaires de France, 1954.

Vitoria, Francisco. *Political Writings*, edited by Anthony Pagden and Jeremy Lawrence. Cambridge: Cambridge University Press, 1991.

Vuillemin, Jules. *Mathématiques et metaphysique chez Descartes*. Paris: Presses Universitaires de France, 1960.

Wolf, A., ed. *The Correspondence of Spinoza*. New York. Russell & Russell, 1966.

Wotton, William. *A defense of the Reflections Upon Ancient and Modern Learning*. London: T. Goodwin, 1705.

Wyrick, Deborah Baker. *Jonathan Swift and the Vested Word*. Chapel Hill: The University of North Carolina Press, 1988.

Zac, Sylvain. *Spinoza et l'Interpretation de l'Écriture*. Paris: Presses Universitaires de France, 1965.

Index